PET LIBRARY

Goldfish

Guide

PET LIBRARY

Goldfish Guide

by Dr Yoshiichi Matsui

**Professor of Fish Culture
Kinki University
Japan**

with a section on Koi
Takayoshi Kumagai
Associate Professor—Applied Zoology
Keio University
Japan

**Edited and with a chapter on
Goldfishkeeping in Great Britain
Captain L. C. Betts, MBE**
President of the
Goldfish Society of Great Britain

THE PET LIBRARY LTD

The Pet Library Ltd.,
Subsidiary of Sternco In-
dustries Inc., 600 South
Fourth Street, Harrison,
N.J. Exclusive Canadian
Distributor: Hartz Moun-
tain Pet Supplies Limited,
1125 Talbot Street, St.
Thomas, Ontario, Canada.
Exclusive United King-
dom Distributor: The Pet
Library (London) Ltd.,
30 Borough High Street,
London S.E. 1.

Printed in the Netherlands

ISBN 0-87826-011-0

Table of Contents

cover picture: Lionhead (Ranchū)

Dr Matsui's Genetic Chart, showing how the different varieties of Japanese goldfish developed.

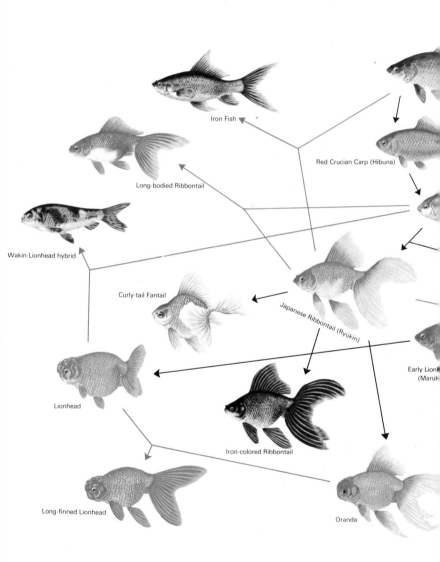

Iron Fish

Red Crucian Carp (Hibuna)

Long-bodied Ribbontail

Wakin-Lionhead hybrid

Curly-tail Fantail

Japanese Ribbontail (Ryūkin)

Lionhead

Early Lion (Maruk

Iron-colored Ribbontail

Long-finned Lionhead

Oranda

The red lines indicate crossing; the black lines, direct mutation.

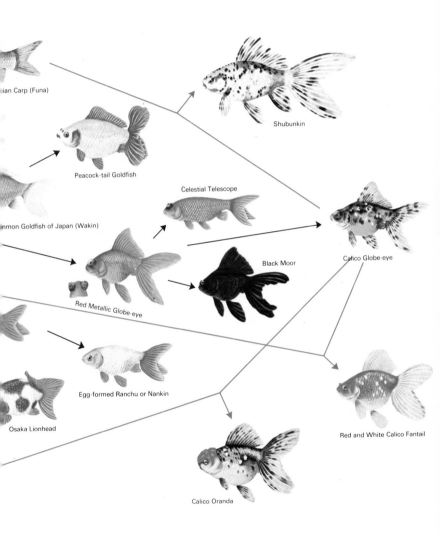

...ian Carp (Funa)

Peacock-tail Goldfish

Shubunkin

...nmon Goldfish of Japan (Wakin)

Celestial Telescope

Red Metallic Globe-eye

Black Moor

Calico Globe-eye

Egg-formed Ranchu or Nankin

Osaka Lionhead

Red and White Calico Fantail

Calico Oranda

COURTESY OF THE CONSULATE GENERAL OF JAPAN

Preface

It is a curious anomaly that despite the work on goldfish done in the Orient extending over many hundreds of years, little information has reached the Western Hemisphere. Extensive research into records has revealed only the barest minimum of data, and the West for its part has had to learn for itself the hard way. It is therefore a surprise and a pleasure to receive from Dr Matsui an authoritative contribution which helps to fill the gap. To European and English-speaking peoples the identification of the species and the translation of the oriental names will fill a long-felt want, whilst the background of explanation on where and how the fishes first came into being will make for a better understanding between East and West in the universal cult of the goldfish.

Captain Leonard C. Betts, MBE
Woodmansterne, England

◀   The peaceful beauty of Japan. People come to the lovely Kinkakuji Temple in Kyoto to feed the goldfish in the lake, observe nature and meditate.

Extracts from mural painted on silk in the 18th century by an anonymous Chinese artist. The piece belongs to the collections of *Ministre Dertin*. The most beautiful specimens of these fish have been reproduced by Billarden de Sauvigny in his "History of the Dorados of China."

I   Introduction

There is a song familiar to all children of Japan,

Oh, my lovely goldfish in your beautiful golden dress,
As you waken gently I'll feed you morsels tenderly,
Oh, my lovely golden pet.

This nursery rhyme makes the goldfish an early friend to all Japanese children, and it is a rare household indeed that has not had goldfish in residence at some time.

Perhaps because our memories of goldfish are associated with our peaceful childhood days, we always remember them with pleasure. In the harsher adult world, the popularity of the goldfish almost seems to be a barometer of a nation's fortunes and spirits. As might be expected, the low point in goldfish culture and appreciation in Japan was reached in the sorry days of the war. The tempo of daily life did not lend itself to the contemplation of graceful fishes gliding through peaceful waters. Even the tranquil ponds devoted to goldfish rearing seemed out of place in those martial times, and moreover, wherever possible they were converted into rice fields to meet the increasing demands of the war.

In the United States the aquarium hobby remained active

throughout the war, perhaps because the quiet, relaxed manners of the goldfish had a soothing effect. After the war, interest in fish increased tremendously, to the point where today it is the third largest hobby in the USA, surpassed only by golf and fishing.

When one thinks of Japanese goldfish, a picture of exotic and rare fishes may come into mind, because it might be imagined that the average Japanese has only beautiful specimens kept under ideal conditions; but this is not the case. As in most Western countries, goldfish are too often considered an expendable pet, so the major part of the domestic Japanese goldfish trade is devoted to the less expensive and hardier varieties. The Wakin, a fish corresponding closely, but not exactly, to the type called "Common Goldfish" in America and Europe, and the Ryūkin,

During the summer, rice paddies are often pressed into service as goldfish rearing ponds. The fish are removed before the water is drained in the late fall.

the Japanese Fantail, are the two types most popular in Japan and account for the overwhelming majority of all fishes sold. The low cost and ready availability of the popular varieties, as well as the myth that goldfish are by nature delicate and their early deaths are to be expected, may account for the scant attention given their needs. This may give people the feeling, "Oh well, they won't survive long anyway, so why bother?" Fortunately, goldfish are rather hardy creatures, and if their basic needs are met, can be kept for twenty years or more. Life expectancy varies with the

A display of goldfish in front of a large department store in Japan. As is common with many Japanese displays, a good many of the tanks are arranged so that the fish are viewed only from above.

different races and types of goldfish, but even in the short-lived varieties, a life span of five or six years should be expected if reasonable care is given to the fish.

This is the "fish that won the West." More common, everyday goldfish like this one are sold than all the other types put together.

II Goldfish History

The Crucian Carp is the common ancestor of all goldfish. It may be difficult to believe that this drab fish is the rootstock from which all the many varieties of shapes and colors of fancy goldfish are descended, but almost all varieties of goldfish prove their common ancestry by reverting to Crucian Carp-like fishes in a very few generations when left unattended by man.

Extracts from a "roll" painted on silk in the 18th century by an anonymous Chinese artist.

Reversion to Type

Examples of this reversion to type can be found in those parts of the world where Crucian Carp are not indigenous. In ponds and rivers where goldfish have been liberated they have multiplied. In each succeeding generation, the formerly domestic pets, now gone wild, increasingly resemble their Crucian Carp ancestors. Over a period of generations, it is hard to distinguish these wild goldfish from those fishes which have never been domesticated by man.

Interestingly enough, however, some populations of wild goldfish seem to remain stable in appearance for a number of generations, and may even resist this reversion to the ancestral form. For example, there are ponds around New York City which have vigorous strains of Comet Goldfish equal to, or better than, many being raised by commercial breeders. While the characteristics of the Comet strain may hold out against the inevitable pressure of nature for a number of years, other strains which would also seem to be well adapted to existing on their own, without man's care, soon revert to the wild gray fishes from which they have been developed.

Shubunkins are a good example of a type which hurries to don its ancestral habit. If several pairs of Shubunkins are released into a pond, the first generations will show the expected proportion of one-half Shubunkin, one-quarter scaleless fish, and one-quarter common scaled fish, that is, with guanophores. In the second generation, wild gray color will outnumber the other two types, and in the third generation only an occasional fish will deviate from the wild gray color.

Trying to thwart nature in her unceasing effort to return goldfish to their natural form is one of the major tasks of the goldfish breeder.

Natural Mutations

Natural mutations of Crucian Carp gave rise to the first fish we would recognize as goldfish. By selecting these desirable mutants and breeding them together, it was possible to produce a good percentage of young fish with the desired characteristics of the parent fish. These early races probably varied little from the wild fish except for color.

The basic principles of genetics were followed by the early breeders of goldfish centuries before Mendel set down his laws. It was an example of a pragmatic approach, a trial-and-error method which gave good results. This is not to downgrade Mendel's work; it has been estimated that these centuries of work could be accomplished in slightly more than one person's lifetime today by taking advantage of our modern knowledge of genetics. This may or may not be so, because such a theory does not take into account the necessity of having the good fortune to first have the new mutations appear spontaneously.

Chinese Origin

When did the first fish we would recognize as a goldfish come into being? There is no clear record of this, but it is agreed that the first goldfish was found in China, that this fish came about through a spontaneous mutation and that it was then cultivated

Japanese artwork by Tatsunobu Kitao (1764) depicting Korean Goldfish and Spatterdock.

This picture of geisha girls feeding their goldfish with chopsticks was painted in 1771 by Harunobu Suzuki in the Ukiyoe style, an art movement of that time. It appeared in the book, "Mirror of Fair Women of Yoshiwara," published in Japan, 1776.

and developed in other shapes by man. The time is generally put in the Sung era, which would be about, or slightly before, the year AD 1000, although old poetry circa AD 800 does mention them.

Two areas of China, the districts of the Che Chiang Chen and Chiang Su Cheng, compete for the honor of having produced the first red Crucian Carp.

In Japan and Europe

The date of the arrival of the first goldfish in Japan from China is somewhat indefinite, but it is fairly certain that they were established in Japan by 1500. The reports of Chinese goldfish being transported to Europe are more definite, and there are records of importations in 1611, 1691 and 1728. In Europe, some success was met in breeding the goldfish, but it is unlikely that any of their descendants are alive today, except in the form of Crucian Carp-like fish which may exist in the wild state.

And America

Goldfish reached America from Japan in 1876 and found a permanent home. Early American fanciers took great care of the specimens which they received. These were excellent examples, which would be esteemed in any company of the best oriental fish even today. Later, interest waned and these beautiful strains were for the most part lost. Today the bulk of the more fancy varieties in the United States are imported fish, since few American breeders attempt to raise any quantity of the rarer and more exotic types. Commercial grade fish are, however, bred and sold in great numbers, and are never in short supply.

A cycle of a sort has been completed in the USA, for goldfish gone wild are sought after as food fish, although when they are marketed to become the entree on someone's table they are usually sold under a local name. In the statistics put out by the United States Government on the freshwater fisheries, goldfish are listed under the heading "Annual Catch." Lake Erie and the Potomac River yield goldfish in commercial quantities for sale as food fishes, although by far the greater part of the catch from these bodies of water go into dog and cat food.

An Oranda used as an illustration in an essay about Nagaskai by Kai Hirokawa published in 1800.

In China, the Crucian Carp is one of the most popular food fishes.

The Scientific Name

The goldfish was first described and named in "Systema Naturae" (1758) as *Cyprinus auratus*.

In 1832, Nilsson established a new genus for it, *Carassius*, and separated *Cyprinus* and *Carassius*.

Cuvier and Vaeciennes in 1842 named the goldfish *Carassius auratus*. So, according to the international rules of zoological nomenclature, the goldfish is *Carassius auratus* and the scientific name for the Crucian Carp is *Carassius carassius*. Actually, since Crucian Carp and goldfish are identical, they should have the same scientific name, or alternatively goldfish should be *Carassius carassius*, var. *auratus*. But traditionally *Carassius auratus* is used for goldfish and *Carassius carassius* for Crucian Carp.

Goldfish in Japan

Goldfish first came to Japan as pets for the aristocracy and the wealthy. One reason that they were limited to these select groups of people is that they were too expensive to buy, since all were imported from China and there were few specimens available. Another reason is that the goldfish was considered too regal to be kept as a pet by the common people.

At first the goldfish was considered too regal to be kept as a pet by the common people.

Royal Fish

In those days, Japan was ruled to a large extent by Shōguns, powerful military governors whose territories were known as "Shogunates." An interesting document dating from 1694 and dealing with the attitude of the rulers to the keeping of the goldfish has been preserved from the Tokugawa Shogunate; this was known as the "Era of Genroku." It seemed that the raising of expensive goldfishes was becoming too popular, so the Tokugawa Shogunate forbade their cultivation on the grounds that it was a frivolous luxury. In Edo City (now Tokyo), which was the Shogunate capital, the idea that goldfish were a luxury died out, and we know that by the seventh year of the Bunsei era (1824), it was accepted that everyone could keep goldfish.

As the keeping of goldfish became more and more popular, goldfish fairs where the fish were exhibited in competition were held. They had their ups and downs in popularity, and eventually most of them were discontinued. However, some of these old fairs have a continuous history down to the present day; for example, one of those started in 1885 is still being held in Tokyo.

Even as the popularity of the formal shows at fairs declined, more people than ever started to keep goldfish. There were

Thousands of people attended this goldfish show at a large department store in Japan.

always seasonal ups and downs; for example, spring and summer found enthusiasm at a high point, while interest lessened during the colder seasons. Since goldfish were generally kept outdoors, it would be natural to expect their popularity to fluctuate. In the garden pools the cold weather made the fish inactive, and usually there were no proper facilities in the average household for bringing them indoors and keeping them properly. In recent years inexpensive aquarium equipment such as air pumps, heaters and filters has become available, so that goldfish can be enjoyed in all seasons, with the result that the demand for them is constant.

T. KUMAGAI

The entries in a local Japanese show. Fish are judged from above for form and color. All containers must be uniform. The banners represent awards.

Selling

Perhaps a few words on the ways goldfish have been sold in Japan would be of interest. When goldfishes were first produced in quantity, the breeders had the double job of first raising the fish and then selling them to individuals. As a railway network spread over Japan, the goldfish market was extended and it became necessary to separate the jobs of the seller and the breeder. Goldfish peddlers who picked up their fishes at the railroad station and then hawked them up and down the street became a common sight. The goldfish peddler made his rounds with two wooden tubs balanced on his shoulders on a "tenbin" stick, calling "Kin-gyō (goldfish), Kin-gyō." In recent years, the peddler with his tenbin stick is a rare sight, but there are still a few peddlers who equip a bicycle with a rear car and pedal through the streets selling their fishes. A business depression meant more goldfish peddlers on the streets, but now, fortunately, times have changed and for the most part the goldfish peddler has become just a memory. Today, if one wants to buy a goldfish the best places are the flower shops and the glass and china stores, as well as the many pet shops.

Major Centers

The major goldfish producing areas of Japan are the Prefectures of Nara, Aichi and Tokyo.

In Nara, goldfishkeeping was mainly limited to the samurai, or warrior class. After the Meiji restoration era, the samurai were no longer privileged class and had to look for ways of supporting themselves and their families. Having had no training other than that of the warrior, many tried to turn what had been a hobby into a livelihood.

Tokyo has a history of goldfish as old as that of Nara. In the early days, fish farms were found in what were then outlying areas but which are now in the bustling center of Tokyo. Growing rapidly, the city forced its fish farms to keep moving to the newer outskirts. Today, however, even in outlying areas the ponds are being filled in for residential areas. With no new pond lands available, the Tokyo area has undoubtedly reached its peak as a goldfish producing center.

A popular children's sport in Japan. The net, which is made of paper, is purchased for about five cents. The child gets to keep all the fish he can catch before the paper disintegrates.

Preparing fish for shipment at a goldfish farm. The air is squeezed out of the bag and replaced with oxygen so as to increase the length of time that the goldfish can travel.

Several bags of goldfish are packed into a heavily waxed, double carton which protects them from leakage and temperature changes.

In Yatomi City of Aichi Prefecture, the goldfish industry started later than those in the Nara and Tokyo areas. The Yatomi district is located near the lower reaches of the Kiso River and was a region once given over to forestry and agriculture. Goldfish raising started out as a farmer's sideline. The Nagoya industrial area now encroaches upon what had been farm and forest, and as a result farms are being rapidly bought up for new housing. Pollution of the water by industrial sewage further reduces the capacity of this area to produce goldfish. In spite of diminishing land and a lack of pure water, this district, because of its favorable climate, ranks second in Japan, ahead of Tokyo and only behind Nara.

In the major goldfish producing areas, fish are raised mainly in ponds built for that express purpose. In the Saitama Prefecture, the fish farmers have developed an unusual method of raising fish by putting them in flooded fields whose primary use is to grow rice.

World-wide Demand

The demand for Japanese goldfish, both in the domestic and overseas markets, continues to increase. A new European market, especially in France, has been opened up, and this, in addition to the USA, is the main area for export. With the increasing demand, as might be expected, other areas of Japan have turned to raising goldfish, but these new areas limit themselves mainly to producing the types of fish popular on the domestic market, such as the Wakin and the Ryūkin. As in the past, the highly bred fish sent overseas still come from the areas of Nara, Tokyo and Aichi, in that order.

At one time, the exporting of goldfish was quite complicated, involving as it did a journey of weeks on the upper decks of a steamer. The fish had to be cared for constantly and, even with attendance, losses could be heavy. Frequent changes of water in the wooden tubs carrying the fishes were made, and in rough weather there was always the danger that salt water would splash into the tubs and cause trouble. Such an inefficient method of transport could only be justified when prices for the fish that survived were high. But even when they charged high prices, the merchants could not realize much of a profit on the sale of the fish alone. With the ingenuity for which the Japanese businessman is noted, they used the proceeds from the sales to purchase articles manufactured in the countries where they sold the fish. This merchandise was then shipped back to Japan for resale; but as Japan became more industrialized the Japanese started to export those items which the goldfish merchants used to bring back. This meant that a more efficient method of transport had to be developed, since the export of goldfish had to be made profitable on its own. Today, of course, goldfish can be sent by fast jet to any part of the world in a few hours.

Flying Fish

Air transport, however, is expensive, so it was necessary to develop an efficient packaging method for flying the maximum number of fish per pound of air freight. To keep traveling weight as low as possible, the fish are put in plastic bags which contain only the minimum amount of water necessary to keep the fish alive. The bags are filled to capacity with oxygen and then packed in lightweight corrugated cardboard boxes. In the search for ways to increase the payload, it has been found that it is possible to increase the number of fish per bag by putting tranquilizers in the water, and also by packing dry ice in the boxes, although the ice must be kept from direct contact with the plastic bag. The dry ice and tranquilizers reduce the activity of the fish by slowing its metabolism. A lowered metabolism means that the fish require less oxygen, and they also do not foul their water so rapidly.

Improved transport has not, unfortunately, solved all of the problems of the goldfish exporter, because the time allowed for air transport is calculated closely and a delay of a few hours along the way may mean the death of the entire shipment. Also, consignees must be kept informed of the exact time of arrival, and must pick up their shipments promptly. Even after arrival fish can be injured if they are handled by untrained people. These are the difficulties and risks that make goldfish exporting a worrisome business. Since there is still a sellers' market in Japan, most Japanese producers avoid shipping problems by limiting their activities to the domestic market.

The goldfish has travelled a long way from the original "gold" carplike fish to this lovely Azumanishiki or Calico Oranda. "Stoney" was ten inches long and 4 years old at the time this picture was taken in 1964. Imported from Japan, he was raised by Mr and Mrs George Mitchell.

III   Physically Speaking

The approach to the goldfish as a pond fish has influenced the thinking of the Chinese and Japanese. When fishes are viewed mainly from above, the emphasis on fin shapes and color in the dorsal region of the body takes precedence over other considerations. When viewed from all angles the importance of the body shape becomes paramount, since it is only then that such ambiguous definitions as "long" or "short", "rounded" or "pointed" and "broad" or "slim" take on meaning. For example, the height of a dorsal fin or the length of a caudal fin is relative to the body measurement since a shallow body will make a dorsal fin appear higher and a short body will make the caudal fin appear longer. If the goldfish is to be developed to its full potential of beauty the shape of the body is a vital statistic which can be evaluated properly only when viewed from all angles.

How they Swim

The swimming methods of fishes are naturally dictated by their shapes. Goldfish are "spindle-like," the most common of all fish shapes. Of course, the body shapes of some of the fancier goldfish are far removed from the original spindle shape, and some of these fancy varieties, being so round and compressed, do not appear to be relatives of the slimmer members of their family. In one variety, in fact, the body shape has been so altered that they are known as "Egg Fish." The swimming behavior of spindle-shaped fish differs from some other types, which swing or undulate their bodies when swimming. Goldfish propel themselves through the water by use of their body muscles and caudal (tail) fin, while the other fins serve mainly to give direction and stability to their movement.

An active goldfish, such as a small Comet or small Shubunkin, can—while it appears to move much faster—swim between two and three miles per hour, but it can maintain this speed for only a short distance. However, it seems to move much faster because it accelerates so rapidly, reaching top speed in a distance equal to less than its own body length.

The eye sacs of these highly developed Bubble-eye Goldfish are quite fragile. Tanks should be free of objects with sharp points or corners.

RICHARD LAW

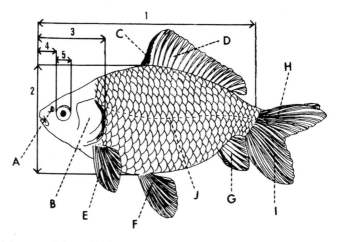

External features of the goldfish.
(1) Body length.
(2) Body depth.
(3) Head length.
(4) Snout length.
(5) Eye diameter.
(A) Narial fold.
(B) Gill cover.
(C) Spiny ray of dorsal fin.
(D) Dorsal fin.
(E) Pectoral fin.
(F) Ventral fin.
(G) Anal fin.
(H) Upper lobe of caudal fin.
(I) Lower lobe of caudal fin.
(J) Lateral line.

Fins

The fin complement of the goldfish is made up of the pectoral fins, the dorsal fin, the anal fin or fins, the caudal or tail fin or fins and the ventral fins (see diagram). The pectoral fins and ventral fins are always paired fins on all goldfish types, and on some types the caudal fins and anal fins are paired as well. The dorsal fins are never paired, and in some types they are absent altogether. Sizes, shapes and carriage of fins should always conform to the standard for the particular variety of goldfish.

Different fins serve different purposes in controlling movement. The pectoral and anal fins control the up and down movements of the fish, and are used to stabilize the fish at a certain depth. Here it should also be mentioned that the air bladder works in conjunction with the pectoral fins and anal fins. To sink lower into the water, the air bladder is contracted; when the air bladder is expanded it helps the fish to rise. The pectoral fins are used to impart upward motion, while the ventral fins are responsible for downward motion. The dorsal and anal fins do not have much relation to the movement of goldfish, and their main function is probably in balancing.

The fin in which the greatest variations are found is the caudal fin, which is most often called the "tail fin" or "tail" for short. There are wild types of caudal fins, triple caudal fins, cherry blossom-like caudal fins, quadruple caudal fins, peacock feather caudal fins, etc. The caudal fins of Shubunkins and Comets differ very little in shape from the wild-type fish except that they are usually longer, as this is the feature for which breeders aim. In goldfish other than Comets and Shubunkins, single caudal fins are considered a serious defect, and these fish are always discarded. In Shubunkin, Comet, Ryūkin and Oranda, the largest caudal fins are generally the most popular, although among serious fanciers too long a tail can be considered an undesirable feature.

The length and shape of the caudal fin influences the swimming motions of the goldfish. This influence is most important in round-bodied fish, particularly the Ranchū, where there is no dorsal fin to help the balance of the fish as it moves through the water. In selecting Ranchū for good caudal fins, there are difficult standards of symmetry to be met, such as the degree of forking between the lobes and the rigidity with which the tail is held. The

The Ranchū, or Lionhead, does not have a dorsal fin. This characteristic is enhanced by selective breeding.

The imbrication, or overlapping of the scales, shows beautifully in this picture of the Wakin, the ordinary Japanese goldfish.

outline of goldfish when swimming is greatly influenced by the degree of triangle from the central horizontal axis and the stiffness at the posterior of the caudal fin. With so many rigid standards to be met, it is easy to see how culling 10,000 young fry might result in only ten fishes being deemed worthy to raise. In goldfishes other than the Ranchū, a slight unevenness of the caudal fins does not affect the swimming configuration so much, so the standards for selection do not have to be nearly so rigid.

Injuries to fins, particularly caudals, can occur easily, especially among the longer-tailed varieties, but if there is no infection following the breaking off of a caudal fin, it will grow back to its former size and shape. There are instances where the tails of long-finned goldfish are deliberately cut short to relieve the fish of the burden of trailing the excessive finnage behind as it swims. This is usually done to a male fish so that he may participate better in a spawning drive.

Scales

The scales covering the goldfish are "imbricated," that is they overlap as beautifully as the roofing tiles on a house. The scales, which start at the head and go back to the region at the base of the tail (known as the caudal peduncle) provide streamlining and protection.

Sometimes, if the scales are injured, new scales will grow back in a reversed direction, resulting in a disorderly appearance. The slime or mucus secretion which covers the scales gives the body a smoother surface and helps protect it against injuries and infections.

The size of the scale varies with the size of the fish. If the scales have a good shape and definition, they are considered to be one of the important points which make up the proper outline, although generally the color of the scales is much more important to the fancier.

Scale Color

The scales on an alevin cannot be seen with the naked eye, but as they grow they become visible. At this stage they are the gray color of the wild ancestral Crucian Carp. Scales of this type are called Futsū Rin, or common scales. These scales are opaque because of the presence of a material called guanine, which is a crystalloid $(C_5H_5N_5O)$. Where the guanine is absent, the scale is transparent. Transparent and common scales are the two types usually found in goldfish, but there is another type called Amitōmei Rin, or net-like transparent scale. A normal scale has black, red, yellow and white pigment cells. In the Crucian Carp, these pigments are all combined in a proportion which produces a dull, unobtrusive color best suited for the fish's protection. Where one of the pigments is missing or is more heavily present than normal, attractive color combinations appear to give the goldfish its peculiar fascination.

There is a common type of goldfish color which is frequently mistaken for scale coloration. This is when the color of the blood shows through from beneath a transparent scale, giving a bluish-purple color which seems to originate in the scale.

Except for the differences of color, or lack of it, the scales of all goldfish are identical in shape and structure, with one exception: the Chinese fish called Chin choo yü, or Pearl Scale. On these, the center of each scale projects outward and is as hard as a samurai's armor. These scales have the shape of a clam shell.

In fishes with horizontally compressed bodies, the rows of scales are sometimes pressed upwards so that they follow a curved rather than a straight line. By examining the curvature of the scale rows, it is possible to tell whether a goldfish is fat due to

An Albino Fantail. Albino goldfish are usually pale gold rather than white. They are distinguished by a lack of pigmentation, including eye pigmentation, which results in the eye appearing red.

heredity or whether its corpulence is due to a fattening diet. Curved scale lines, particularly in the dorsal region above the lateral line, generally indicate that a fish belongs to a short-bodied strain.

Fading Away Change

When the young fish with Futsū Rin, or common scales, are 50 to 60 days old, a change generally begins. This is one of the pleasures anticipated each year by all those who raise goldfish. This is called the "color-fading-away change." As the "color-fading-away change," or decoloring, begins, the Crucian color will turn somewhat blackish. Following this phase, the ventral (lower) area of the fish starts to lighten to an orange-yellow color, which gradually works its way up to the dorsal region. At this time goldfish usually present an unattractive figure, although sometimes the fishes which are turning color can be quite striking if there is a sharp contrast. Often these orange and black fish are sold as a distinct color variety, under the name "Oriole" after the

32

Baltimore Oriole; but the buyer of one of these fishes usually finds that the black soon disappears.

When the black finally disappears, the fish are a yellowish-orange color, but with the passing of time the orange becomes more vivid until it becomes a bright red-orange. In some goldfish, white may be mixed in with this red, and if the red is vivid this makes a pleasing contrast.

Not all young goldfish go through this decoloring phase. Some may never decolor, and others may take two to three years. If the decoloring does not occur satisfactorily, the parent fish are suspect and usually discarded, unless they have features other than color which are desirable. The best commercial hatcheries boast that through selection they have developed strains which will average 97 per cent or better decoloring after five months.

Decoloring occurs among common scaled, or, as they are sometimes known, metallic fishes. In the case of the transparent-scaled fishes such as the triple color Demekin and the Shubunkin, the young fish never have the wild Crucian color. At the outset, they are a light color, very often white; this deepens day by day until finally they become multicolored fish with mixtures of red, white, black, yellow and blue.

The beautiful colors of the goldfish are dependent on the type and distribution of the pigment cells, and on the presence and distribution of the reflecting body and scale layers. In the common scaled goldfish, there are black and yellow pigment cells. When the fish decolors, it means that the black cells disappear, leaving the fish with its yellowish orange pigment. Some are a pale yellow, while in others the color becomes so deep that they could be considered red. Various factors, such as water chemistry, light, heat, food and, of course, genetic makeup, can influence color intensity.

Because of disease or injury, the tips of the fins may turn black, but this is not a permanent color, and when the fish recovers the black will fade away. Black color can also show up on the fins of goldfish that have no record of being injured. Here it seems to be some major change in environment which causes the fish to take on black, although the reasons for this are not definitely known.

If fish which have been kept indoors or in a shady place are exposed to bright sunlight, the fins and sometimes even the entire body can turn black; but this does not seem to indicate any harm.

Some Orandas, like this Goosehead Azumanishiki, are bred to have the coverage primarily on the top of the head like a high cap. This is common among Chinese Orandas.

The fish are called "sunburned," as the black color is a transient one which disappears in a few weeks. This sunburn phenomenon occurs only in certain ponds, and not every year even in these. Occasionally fish are trapped in shallow water which is exposed to direct sunlight and high temperatures, even up to 100°F. These will turn white and appear scalded.

The Head

Normally the head of a goldfish is a narrow delta, but goldfish can have broad heads or any variation in between. In general, it can be said that the head of a goldfish should be well shaped and in proportion to the size of the body of the fish. The fine points of head shape will be mentioned in the description of the various races of goldfish, but here let us touch briefly on the unusual heads in the Ranchū, Oranda and the Hanafusa.

The heads of Ranchūs and Orandas have coverings which consist of thickened tissue. These coverings are made up of overlapping small wen-like growths which are the distinguishing feature of the species. A full-hooded fish would have "wens" on top of its head, on its cheeks and on the sides of the mouth. These full coverings are sought after in the Ranchū, which is known as the "Lionhead." Some Orandas are bred to have coverage primarily on the top of the head so that it rides there like a high cap.

Hanafusa (Pompon) is a variety in which the nasal appendages are greatly enlarged and tufted.

Eyes

The eyes of a goldfish are similar to those of most other vertebrates. However, as they cannot open and shut the iris, nor expand and contract the lens, they are believed to be somewhat nearsighted.

When goldfish are searching for food, their sense of smell seems to be more important than their sight. The four principal types of eyes found are the normal small eye, telescope eye, up-turned telescope or celestial eye and bubble eye. Variations from the normal are ornamental only and serve no practical purpose. They undoubtedly reduce the vision of the fishes.

The goldfish appears to be capable of seeing the same range of colors as a human, and can distinguish shapes and sizes.

KLAUS PAYSAN

The enormous development of the eyes of the Celestial Telescope is only ornamental. It serves no practical purpose; in fact, it reduces the fish's ability to see.

Hearing

Goldfish have no external ears, but they do have inner ones. These inner ears contain lymph and will pick up sound vibrations in the water. Goldfish also feel vibrations in the water caused by sound or pressure waves impinging on its lateral line. Airborne sounds probably do not penetrate the water too well, but vibrations on the ground near the water are transmitted and felt quite plainly. For example, when you walk to your aquarium, it is doubtful that your fishes *hear* your footsteps, but they can detect the vibration as your foot strikes the ground.

Memory

The sense of sight and sound, as well as memory, can be demonstrated in goldfish if they are given some training. For example, if you tap at the pond's edge each day before feeding, the goldfish will soon respond to the tapping and gather at their feeding spot even before any food is put into the water. Or they can be trained by swirling the water before feeding. After a time, the fish will respond to the sight of the fishkeeper as he nears the pond, since his presence means mealtime. If fishes are fed irregularly, they are likely to dart away when anyone approaches.

Gills

The bony plates on either side of the goldfish's head, commonly

T. KUMAGAI

At Kōriyama, little old ladies sort goldfishes, using a series of white enamel pans. The fish shows up starkly and the bowl's shape provides maximum air surface in relation to depth.

referred to as gills, are really gill covers, or more technically, opercula (singular: operculum). The gills themselves are filamentous membranes located just behind the opercula, which protect them. Each of the gill filaments that are attached to the gill arches is richly supplied with blood vessels.

The heart pumps the blood directly to the gills, and from there throughout the body. The circulation is sluggish, with a pulse (heartbeat) of 20 to 50 beats per minute. The rate is dependent on the ambient temperature and activity of the fish.

Water is taken in through the mouth and passed over the gills; by osmosis, carbon dioxide and other wastes are discharged from the blood, and oxygen dissolved in the water is absorbed into the bloodstream through the delicate membrane of the filaments.

Goldfish have teeth in the throat with which they chew their food, but this does not impede the flow of water from mouth to gills.

When the water is deficient in oxygen, or is polluted because of decomposing matter such as uneaten food, the fishes will tend to congregate at the surface, because it is here that gaseous exchanges between the water and the atmosphere take place most rapidly. The gills will open wide at each inhalation and the effort of breathing often makes little popping noises and bubble formations. Should this occur, increase aeration and, if possible, change part of the water. (See section on Water Changes.)

Reproductive Organs

The ovaries of the female lie in the upper part of the body cavity, more or less parallel to the kidneys. The eggs are first discharged into a hollow central cavity of the ovary and then passed to the exterior through special ducts.

The testes of the male fishes occupy a position in the body comparable to that of the ovaries of the female, and like them are provided with special ducts to lead the sex products from the body.

When a fish spawns, its sex products are passed out through the anus, the same opening through which solid and liquid wastes are excreted.

The size of the reproductive glands increases tremendously as spawning time approaches (especially the ovaries, which in extreme cases can make up 25 to 30 per cent of the body weight)

Taste

Very little is known about the sense of taste in goldfishes. In the presence of an ample supply of food, they will tend to choose certain things in preference to others; however, when they are hungry they will swallow almost anything. In addition to tasting with the mouth, like most fishes they have sensory organs which seem to function much like taste sensors located over the body. Fishes are capable of detecting the presence of very minute quantities of a substance dissolved in water, in some cases as little as one part in 100 million, although exactly how they detect these substances is not yet clear.

Smell

This is probably tied in with the senses described in the preceding paragraph. Fishes do have nostrils, but they are not connected with the mouth or throat the way ours are. They are a U-shaped passage, lined with sensitive cells which detect the presence of odors or substances in the water. A fish's sense of smell, taste, hearing, lateral line sensation and possibly other sensory receptors with which we are not familiar all work closely together to keep him aware of his environment.

Sleep

As fishes have no eyelids, it was once taken for granted that they did not sleep; however, sleep is a condition of the mind and is not really dependent on eyelids. Goldfish can and do rest, usually when the tank or pool is dark. Each fish will have its own resting place, to which it repairs as the light dims.

Even when the fish is kept under artificial light continually, it will stop and rest, usually in a favorite place on the bottom, sometimes for several hours. It seems to lose contact with its surroundings to such an extent that it does not respond readily to noise or even a light touch. If the disturbance is strong enough, the fish appears startled and confused for a few minutes, but it gradually returns to its resting state.

IV Races or Varieties of Goldfish

The Catalogue of Japanese Goldfish
by Takayoshi Kumagai

Japanese	Chinese	English
鮒 / Funa	鯽 魚 / Chi Yü	Crucian Carp or Silver Carp
緋鮒 / Hibuna	金 鯽 / Chin Chi	Red Crucian Carp / Prototype of Goldfish
和金 / Wakin	芽 魚 / Tsuo Yü (Two-lobed)	Common Goldfish or False Wakin
	文 魚 / Wan Yü (Tri-lobed one)	Wakin
琉金 / Ryūkin	文 魚 / Wen Yü	Fantail, Veiltail
	燕 尾 / Yian Wei	Ribbontail
鉄魚 / Tetsugyo		Long-finned Crucian Carp or Iron Fish
鉄尾長 / Tetsuonaga		Iron-colored Ribbontail
キャリコ / Calico	五 彩 文 魚 / Wu Tsai Wenfü	Calico (Macaroni, matt.)
朱文金 / Shubunkin	朱 文 金 / Chin Wen Chin	Shubunkin
出目金 / Demekin	竜 眼 竜 頭 / Lung Yü or Lung Chin	Telescope-eyed or Globe-eye
オランダ獅子頭 / Oranda Shishigashira	紅 帽 子 / Hon mao Tze 花 帽 子 / Non Mao Tze	Oranda
東 錦 / Azumanishiki	五 彩 高 頭 / Wu Tsai Kao Tou	Calico Oranda or Ayumanishiki
頂 天 眼 / Chōtengan	朝 天 竜 / Chiao Tien Lung 望 天 竜 / or Wan Tien Lung	Celestial Telescope
コメット / Comet		Comet
サバオ / Sabao		Swallow-tailed Ryūkin or Mackerel tail (Swallow-tailed Wakin)
山形金魚 / Yamagata Kingyo		
大阪蘭鋳 / Osaka Ranchu		Osaka Ranchu

Japanese	Chinese	English
蘭 鋳 / Ranchū	獅 子 頭 / Shu Tze Tou	Lionhead, Bramble Head or Ranchū
丸 金、弘 魚 / Jikin, Kujyaku		Peacock-tail Goldfish or Jikin
土 佐 金 / Tosakin		Curly-tail Fantail or Tosakin
南 金 / Nankin		Egg-formed Ranchū or Nankin
和 尾 沼 / Watonao		Long-bodied Ribbontail
津 軽 錦 / Tsugarunishiku		Long-formed Ranchū
舒 錦 / Shūkin		Shūkin
金 蘭 子 / Kinranshi		Kanranshe or Wakin-Ranchū Hybrid

The Catalogue of Chinese Goldfish
by Takayoshi Kumagai

Japanese	Chinese	English
珍 珠 鱗 / Chinshurin	珍 珠 魚 / Chin Chro Yü 珍 珠 鱗 / Chin Chro Lin	Pearl Scale
水 泡 眼 / Suihgan	水 泡 眼 / Shui Pao Ipen	Bubble-eye
絨 玉 / Hanaguen	絨 球 魚 / Rrun Chin Yü	Pompon or Narial Bouquet
反 鰓 / Makiera	翻 鰓 / Fan Sai	Outturned Operculum
丹 頂 / TanchE	紅 頭、鶴 頂 紅 / Hon Tou、Ho Tien Hon 元 宝 紅 / Yuen Bao Hon	Redcap
茶 金、唐 錦 / Chakin, Karanishiki	錦 魚、褐 魚 / Ten Yü, Ho Yü	Brown Goldfish
青 文 魚 / Seitsugyo, Nagezome	青 文 魚 / Chin Wen Yü 藍 文 魚 / Lang Wen Yü	Blue Goldfish

THIS CHART OF CHINESE AND JAPANESE GOLDFISH WAS PREPARED BY TAKAYOSHI KUMAGAI AND PRINTED HERE BY PERMISSION OF THE AUTHOR.

THE ENGLISH EQUIVALENTS AND PRONUNCIATIONS ARE BASED ON THE LATEST AND MOST UP TO DATE INFORMATION.

There are many varieties of goldfish which show up from time to time. When a desirable characteristic appears in a fish and it can be bred true to type over many generations, the fish showing these characteristics can be considered a race or variety of goldfish. Race is perhaps a better word to use than variety, since it has more of an implication of permanence. While there may be variations among the offspring which do not meet the standards for the type, there should always be a predictable percentage of young fish which do.

The countries which have originated races of goldfish are China, Japan and the United States of America. Since the author's genealogical studies have been restricted to Japanese goldfish, it would seem proper that we start off with a consideration of the goldfish races of Japan. For races known and named in the English-speaking world, we will use the English name and give the

This egg shaped Oranda, raised in England, is so finely developed that it looks almost artificial.

Japanese equivalent. For those not named in English, we will use the Japanese word, spelled phonetically.

According to old records and prints, the original races were apparently Wakin, Hibuna and Maruko, which was an early type of Ranchū. The fact that these races are comparatively easily transported lends support to the theory that these were the first fishes to arrive in Japan. Ryūkins were imported about 1800, followed by Demekins in 1895. All of these races have subsequently produced other varieties, and in Japan today there are more than twenty varieties. These may be classified according to their origin as follows:

Races imported from China: Wakin, Maruko, Ryūkin, Demekin.
Varieties produced in Japan:

(a) By selection from prototypes: Jikin, Nankin, Tosakin, Tetsuonaga, Ōsaka Ranchū, Hanafusa, Oranda Shishigashira.

(b) By crossing between prototypes: Kinranshi, Shubunkin, Shūkin, Calico, Azumanishiki.

Races in Japan:

(a) Common Goldfish of Japan (Wakin)—This race, the most common and most primitive, has short fins and a rather slender body for a goldfish. Wakin is a very hardy fish and the least expensive of all varieties. Its body shape closely resembles the Crucian Carp, ancestor of all the races.

The scales are cycloid and the normal ones have iridocyst or guanine layers.

The young fish are colored brownish-blue-black, which is known as iron color. With development, the color gradually fades away and the fish turn yellow, orange, white or an orange-white piebald color. The decoloration is affected by the physical condition of the fish, as well as by environmental conditions. The start of the decoloring phase varies between individuals and different strains, and may vary from 50 days to more than 170 days after the fish hatch.

Since Wakins do not have showy finnage, the one feature for which they should be bred is intensity of color. The all-white or pearl Wakin is considered to be an inferior fish.

Wakins are very active fish and should not be kept with some of the more delicate varieties, such as Demekin. The Wakins would monopolize all of the food, and might harass the Demekins by pecking at their fins or eyes and generally roughing them up. Wakins will grow quite large, and can measure seven or eight inches when they are 3 years old.

The Ryūkin originally was bred in China, but reached the United States via Japan. This High Humpbacked type is bred primarily on the west coast of the USA.   JOHN H. TASHJIAN

The Wakin is the most popular of all goldfish in Japan but it is rarely seen outside of its homeland.

(b) The First True Goldfish (Hibuna)—These seem to be a variety of wild goldfish resembling the Crucian Carp even more so than the Wakin. The color of Hibunas is not as vivid as that of Wakins, and is usually a rather yellowish-orange. Hibunas go through the same decoloration phase as Wakins do, but the process usually begins much later, sometimes in the third year.

At present, this race is quite rare, and many of the so-called Hibunas may be Wakins with a single tail, or a hybrid of Wakin and the Crucian Carp (Funa). Wild fish which are descended from domesticated goldfish might very well be indistinguishable from the true Hibuna.

(c) Peacock Tail (Jikin, Rokurin, Shachi or Kujyaku)—This is a very old race of goldfish which was developed from the Wakin. It has the characteristic Wakin body shape, although slightly more compressed vertically and thicker in the abdominal region. All of the fins are short. The distinguishing characteristic of this

A Jikin, or Peacock Tail Goldfish, rare even in Japan.

The characteristic tail shape of the Jikin.

DR Y. MATSUI

An elegant female Ryūkin. This variety can be kept easily, even by the beginner.

race is the caudal fin, called "kuzyaku-wo," peacock tail. Viewed from the rear, the tail is X-shaped, and from this view the caudal peduncle is broad and covered with small scales. The axis of the tail is almost perpendicular to the body axis. It is interesting to note that only about forty per cent of the progeny of even an apparently pure breed that has undergone rigorous selection for 50 to 60 generations will breed true to type for the peacock tail.

The most desired specimens of this race have red lips and fins, while the rest of the body is white. Such fish are called Rokurin, but fish with the proper markings are very rare. Artificial methods

A Telescope Black Moor. The dead-black velvety color with no trace of brass is the most desirable.

are often resorted to to get the coloring, either through the use of various acids or by operating on the fish.

The figure a goldfish makes as it swims through the water is just as important for proper appreciation as is the color and form. The tail sticking out at right angles gives the Jikin its own distinct swimming motion. Sometimes the tail is likened to the propeller on a ship.

(d) Japanese Fantail (Ryūkin)—These are the second most popular goldfish in Japan. The body is short and somewhat compressed. All the fins should be long, so this race is sometimes called "Onaga," which means long-tailed. The tail is long and like a veil. The paired-tail fish Yotsu-wo and Mitsu-wo are the most common, but some of these fish have a single tail and are called Hukinagashi, or banner-tail. The single-tailed fish are sometimes given a separate classification and called Nymphs, but these are not really a separate race.

Ryūkins have the same body colors as do Wakins, and they go through a similar decoloration phase. However, the Ryūkins tend to start their decoloring later than do Wakins.

Ryūkins are very elegant goldfish, and fortunately not in the least expensive. In recent years the caudal fin seems to be getting somewhat shorter on the fish that are seen on the market. We should never have to fear that this variety will be in short supply, since it is one that the fish farmers are always eager to raise. Efforts put into the cultivation of Ryūkin are well rewarded, since the fish are hardy and breed true to type in large proportion, producing many saleable fish.

Before leaving the Ryūkins, we should mention a fish that is probably descended from them, called the Yamagata Goldfish (from the Yamagata Prefecture). The bodies of these fish are of the Ryūkin shape, but they always have single caudals which are long and broad. This strain seems to be very resistant to cold water. It is sometimes called Sabao, or Mackerel Tail.

(e) Telescope-eyed Goldfish (Demekin)—The body and fins of Demekins are comparatively short, as they were when first imported from China, although in recent years many specimens with relatively long fins have been noted both in Japan and China.

As the name indicates, the distinguishing feature of these fish is the large, protruding eyes. These may vary in shape from roundish to almond shaped. This eye characteristic first appears when the fish is about a month old, and the eyes continue to get bigger as the fish grows. The rate of eye development varies greatly from fish to fish. Sometimes only one eye will develop while the other remains normal, or only partially protrudes. These are considered inferior fish, as symmetry is always required in telescope-eyed fish.

The telescope-eyed fish can be classified in three varieties:

The Red Telescope-eyed Goldfish (Aka Demekin), also called Red Metallic Globe-eye, has ordinary scales and goes through the decoloring phase.

The Black Telescope-eyed Goldfish or Black Moor (Kuro Demekin) has ordinary scales which should have a deep black color; this comes about from an excess of melanic pigment deposited in the scales. This pigment begins to appear about sixty days after hatching, and varies in its intensity from fish to fish. When the black color is less intense the fish are considered to be inferior, and the best specimens should be a deep blue-black color which covers the entire body, including the ventral area. It is not uncommon for black fish to go into a second color change as they get older, and they may then take on the appearance of the Aka

Demekin. It should be noted that the solid black color appears only on telescope-eyed fish, which would indicate that the gene for black color is linked to that for telescope eye.

The Calico Telescope-eyed Goldfish (Sanshoku Demekin) has

A well developed Lionhead, bred in California. This attractive combination of brassy body with the blood-red hood is the most sought after.   JOHN H. TASHJIAN

ordinary scales and transparent scales mixed in a mosiac form, with the transparent scales scattered among the ordinary ones in a random pattern. It is likely that this variety is a hybrid between a pure transparent-scaled fish and a normal-scaled one. The fish with all transparent scales are rather difficult to rear, and they are no longer found as a pure breed.

The Calico Telescope-eye belongs to a class of fish which do not go through the decoloring phase. Varied and vivid colors are desirable in these fish, with red, blue, white, black, purple and yellowish-brown distributed overall.

(f) Lionhead (Ranchū)—The body of the Ranchū is short, broad and roundish. A distinguishing characteristic of this race is the absence of the dorsal fin; all other fins should be short. The Ranchū is an old race. The evidence given in old prints and scrolls indicates that it originally came from China.

There are four varieties of this race of goldfish—Lionhead, Maruko, Ōsaka and Nankin. The original apparently was the Maruko, which came about as a mutation from the Wakin. The other three types were developed from the Maruko. In all four types, the absence of a dorsal fin is the feature which indicates that they are members of the same race. However, in none of the types is the absence of the dorsal fin a stable characteristic. When 40 per cent of the young in a spawning lack a dorsal fin, this is considered a very good percentage, even in strains which have been bred with care for dozens of generations.

Lionhead Ranchū: The Lionhead is considered the king of the goldfish in Japan. The head is enlarged by a warty excrescence which is an abnormal growth of cuticular tissue and commonly

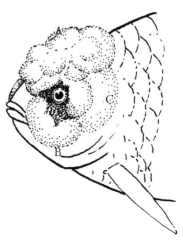

Regions of the goldfish head where growth can occur:
(A) Cap, (B) Cheek,
(C) Opercular region.

called a "hood." In order for the hood to have a place on which to grow and develop properly, the top of the head on the Lion-head has been broadened to give a good base for the hood. This breadth of head is always an important point to look for when selecting young fishes which are to be kept and raised to maturity. The hood is considered to be made up in three sections: the cranial or top of head; infraorbital, or below the eyes; and operculate, which extends over the gill plates. According to the degree of development of the hood in each of these areas, fish are known as:

1. Lionhead (Ranchū), in which the three sections are equally developed.
2. Hi-cap or Goosehead (Tokin), in which the cranial part alone is developed.
3. Swollen-cheeked (Okame), in which the infraorbital and the opercular parts are developed.

A well-developed hood has the appearance of a ripe raspberry, being covered all over with small, round, blisterlike prominences from 0.5 50 1.55 mm in diameter. As a rule, the hood should be visible to the naked eye about one-hundred and twenty days after hatching. Its development depends greatly upon the manner in which the fish are raised. The quality and temperature of the water and the diet all play a part. Although water with some algae growth in it is generally beneficial to gold-fish, it appears that the algae may inhibit the growth of the hood. One method to promote hood growth is to use water which is free from algae, but which has been aged for a day or two in sunlight. Further, in order to keep the water free from algae, it must be changed often and shaded with a blind or screen. A shaded area is also necessary so that the Lionhead can escape from the bright midday sun. Special feeding is also necessary to promote optimum hood growth, and fanciers feed their fish large amounts of *Tubifex* worms and *Chironomus* larvae, popularly known as bloodworms.

Young Lionheads kept under conditions which are suitable for other fishes may never develop the full hood. It is interesting to conjecture why this should be so. One hypothesis is that, if given the opportunity, nature will protect the Lionhead by restricting the growth of a non-functional, purely ornamental structure.

The coloring of Lionheads and all Ranchūs is generally like that of Wakins, but seldom with the intensity of color which is found in the latter. In the best Wakins and Ryūkins, the color can be almost scarlet, but Lionheads are usually metallic gold, although mixed red and white or all white can be found. It is normal for the hood to be the same color as the rest of the body, but some striking specimens have a yellowish-gold body with a red hood, and this contrast gives the fish a very pleasing appearance.

A rare and very beautiful color pattern sometimes found in Lionheads is one in which each scale is rimmed with a color different from the body of the scale.

Standards for judging Lionheads are extremely high, and it is unusual for a fish not to be faulted on one or more points. Tails must be curved properly and held at the correct angle; scales should lie in neat rows and lines and show good definition; the dorsal area must be broad, rounded and smooth, showing no trace of a bump or irregularity; the caudal peduncle should be large and broad, and the body should be symmetrical from any angle. When the fish can pass all of these tests, and also, of course, has a well-developed hood, it is further screened for intensity of color, color patterns, carriage while at rest, carriage while swimming and so on. Just considering the sheer mathematics of it, it is easy to see why there are very few Lionheads that can pass all the tests and why thousands of fish must be gone through and discarded just to find several that are worthy to be raised in the hopes they will develop into future champions.

There are gatherings every year in Japan of people from all parts of the country who are members of the Japan Ranchū Association. The convention with the longest history is the Tokyo Goldfish Appreciation Show, which has met every year since 1889. In Hawaii, there is a branch of the "Ranchū Association of Friends of Similar Tastes," and each year judges from Japan come to their annual exhibitions.

The raising of good Lionheads is a very difficult part of the goldfish hobby, but those who become involved with Lionheads soon ignore other varieties completely.

Maruko Ranchū: The prototype of the Lionhead shows the least development of the Ranchūs and has no puffy growth on its head. Today this type is not being bred, although a fish with no hood development shows up from time to time in batches from other types of Ranchū.

DR Y. MATSUI

The Ōsaka Ranchū is closely related to the Lionhead, but does not have a rasberry head and is much more rounded.

Ōsaka Ranchū: Unlike the Lionhead, the Ōsaka Ranchū does not have a hood. The head is small and pointed to the tip of the mouth. The body shape is the most rounded of all the Ranchū types. The tail is paired and short, and is almost perpendicular to the body axis. The particular plane of the tail and of the body shape gives the Ōsaka Ranchū a distinctive swimming motion, and it oscillates from right to left while moving through the water.

Since Ōsaka Ranchūs were shown competively for many years before competitions for Lionheads were started, it is probable that this is an older variety than the Lionhead. The popularity of the Ōsaka Ranchū has decreased over the years, probably because it does not have a hood, and today there are only a few people who are interested in preserving the race.

Nankin Ranchū: Nankins are raised only in the Shimane district. In appearance they are very close to the prototype fishes that started the Ranchū line. The body shape is somewhat longer than the Lionheads, and the head is small and narrow. This variety does not have any hood development either. The distinguishing feature of the Nankin is its color pattern, which is called "rokurin": a white body with red at the tip of the mouth, on the gill covers and on every fin.

The Nankin is another of those varieties that are not widely distributed and that can usually be found only in the area that has specialized in their breeding.

(g) Celestial (Chōtengan)—Celestials have no dorsal fin and are sometimes called Deme-Ranchū. The name might lead one to assume that they are related to the Ranchūs, but this is not the case. They are derived from the Red Telescope. Thirty Celestials were first brought to Japan about 1903 from China and bred successfully. However, the strain died out in Japan. Chōtengans that are being bred today in Japan are descended from fish that were imported from China after World War II. Interestingly, the Chōtengans that are seen on the market today in Japan resemble the old type, which were short-finned fish, whereas Chinese Chōtengans are often long-finned fish, the tail often being as long as the body. Perhaps these long-tailed fish are more readily

A pair of Orandas (male above) with an unusual dark cap. This type, called Chabōshi, comes from China.

marketable, but whether the new Chinese-style Chōtengan is an improvement is a matter of taste.

The distinguishing feature of the Chōtengan is the upturned eyes, and it is these eyes gazing skyward which gave them the name of "Celestial."

The body shape is long and the usual color is orange-yellow. As with the telescope-eyed fishes, the eyes of the Celestial are normal at birth. The peculiar eye development starts about one-hundred and twenty days after the fish are hatched. Approximately thirty per cent of the young will have the upturned eyes.

In discussing Celestials, the charming fable of how these fish were developed should be mentioned. According to the tale, the fish were kept in covered jars with little slits at the top, and the fish eventually turned their eyes upward to seek out the source of light.

Another explanation of their origin—perhaps one with a little more solid foundation—is that they were developed as a tribute to an ancient Chinese emperor. Whenever he came to admire his fish, he found them gazing up at him adoringly.

In Celestials, the absence of a dorsal fin is, genetically speaking, more stable than in the Ranchū varieties. About sixty per cent of the fishes will breed true for this characteristic.

(h) Oranda (Shishigashira)—This variety has a head like that of the Lionhead Ranchū, although the growth on the cap is usually the most pronounced part of the hood. The body of the Oranda is short, but not as short as either the Fantail or the Lionhead. The fins should be long and showy, and the dorsal fin should always be present. One theory is that the Oranda was developed by crossing the Lionhead and the Fantail, but experiments carried on by the author seem to indicate strongly that the Oranda originated as a mutation from the Fantail. One of the things which led me to this conclusion was that regardless of the number of breedings, no Orandas lacked a dorsal fin, which might have been expected if there were Lionhead ancestors. However, it must be reported that some breeders have found the inheritance of the dorsal fin to be an unstable characteristic in Orandas. Since in the author's experiment the appearance of the dorsal fin was a stable characteristic, it may be that at some time Orandas and Lionheads were crossed, and their offspring have gotten onto the market to confuse the matter.

A Calico Oranda. This fish does not have enough blue to qualify as a top specimen, and in this picture, at least, the rays of the dorsal and pectoral fins appear to be bent.

The best Orandas, as is the case with Lionheads, are raised by amateur fanciers rather than by professional breeders. Probably the reason for this is—as with the Lionheads—that so many fish must be discarded and so much painstaking culling gone through as to make the raising of superior Orandas unattractive economically to the professional.

Orandas come in various colors, and all-red, red and white, orange-yellow, Crucian gray and black varieties are known. In China, other color varieties of Oranda—blue, blue-brown and brown—have been developed.

The head growth of the Oranda is not as pronounced as it is in the best Lionheads, and it usually develops at a later age than does the corresponding growth in Lionheads. While the head growth in Orandas may lag several months behind the development in

Lionheads, caution is advised for all those who would purchase either Orandas or Lionheads for breeding or show purposes. Many times a group of fish who display no signs of any head development will be offered for sale by a dealer. The usual explanation is that the fish are young and that the head has not yet started to develop the characteristic hood. Unless the fish are very young and come from stocks of a known pedigree, fish showing no early signs of a hood should be avoided. Of course, a fully developed fish will be much more expensive than a number of immature specimens, but the additional investment is worthwhile if you want the best in breeding stock.

(i) Calico Oranda (Azumanishiki)—The Japanese name reminds every Japanese of Sumo wrestlers. Although the standard body shape is somewhat more compressed than that of the Oranda, the common name for this fish is Calico Oranda. Like the Oranda, it has a hood development on its head which increases in size with age. Azumanishikis, with their mixture of transparent and normal scales, display an exceptionally beautiful profusion of colors. Good specimens of Azumanishiki can equal the best calico coloring seen on any type of goldfish, with splashes of red, white, black, blue and orange-yellow, sprinkled all over with fine black dots. An especially striking color distribution is a fish with the aforementioned pattern and with a solid black hood.

Azumanishikis are one of the newer varieties of Japanese goldfish. In spite of their beautiful coloration and good hood growth, they seem to be quite hardy and under proper conditions do well outdoors the year round. They are one of the largest varieties of the fancy goldfishes and will grow as large as Orandas.

Azumanishikis have been developed by crossing Orandas and the Calico Telescope-eyed Goldfish (Sanshoku Demekin). This is not a cross which can be developed in a single generation, however, and it took several generations to arrive at the desired combination of characteristics.

(j) Calico—The name "Calico" leaves something to be desired for the next fish we are going to discuss. Ordinarily, Calico brings to mind in goldfish a mixture of many colors, among which blue and black are considered very desirable. In Japan, fish known as "Calico" do not have any blue or black on them normally, but are colored red or dappled red and white. They are hybrid fish, which can be produced in one generation by crossing red Fantails with Calico Telescopes. To differentiate this fish from others that have "Calico" in their name, we call them Calico Fantails. The Calico Fantail very often has a body that is shorter and laterally more compressed than either of its parents. The scales are a

A commercial grade Calico Fantail showing a good blue area.

OZARK FISHERIES

mixture of transparent and normal; the usual arrangement is with the transparently-scaled part of the fish red, and the normal silver-colored scales showing up beautifully against the red background.

A group of Cambridge Blue Shubunkins showing the desired blue coloration.

By breeding Calico Fantails together, it is possible to bypass the limitation of only red or red–and–white dapple coloration. There are now beautiful specimens of Calico Fantails in Japan that have blue, black and other colors mixed through the arrangement of transparent and normal scales. The development of the Calico Fantail of superior coloration is a work of art accomplished mainly by Mr Kichigorō Akiyama, who is a past master at developing goldfish by selective crossings. His work spans three generations of Japanese life, from the Meiji era through the Taishō era, continuing down to the present Shōwa era.

(k) Shubunkin—The Shubunkin is a single-tailed fish that is extremely hardy. It has the same complement of fins as does the wild goldfish, although these should be somewhat longer, with the tips of the caudal fins being rounded. All known colors of the goldfish can appear in the Shubunkin and the colors are varied and intense in good specimens. Blue is considered the most desirable and this should be a bright true blue, not a slate color. The name, itself means "red brocade" or "of many colors with red."

Over the patches of blue coloring there are, ideally, blotches of red, orange, yellow and brown with a stippling of black dots over all of the colors, as if one had flicked a brush of black paint over the fish. All-blue Shubunkins—or even Shubunkins which will breed true for large patches of blue—have long been sought, but so far this goal does not seem to have been reached.

While the Shubunkin is a goldfish of fairly simple shape, and therefore might be thought of as one of the earlier varieties, this does not seem to be the case. Shubunkins, as we know them today, were first bred by Mr Kichigorō Akiyama in 1900. Akiyama developed his Shubunkins by crossing three varieties: the Calico Telescope, the Fork-tailed Wakin and the Hibuna. The author's experiments have shown that Shubunkins can be obtained by a simple cross of Calico Telescopes with Crucian Carps.

(l) Curly-tailed Fantail (Tosakin)—This is a beautiful race of goldfish which is bred in the city of Kōchi and its environs. Tosakins are quite similar to Ryūkins, the main difference being that their fins are a bit shorter and the tail has a characteristic shape, being extended on both sides with its outer rim upturned. Tosakins are probably the result of mutations from the Ryūkins.

At one time Tosakins were quite popular, and competitions for them were held regularly in and about Kōchi city. However, in recent years their popularity has declined, and now there are just a few fanciers who manage to keep this race in existence.

Tosakins are raised in shallow ponds because of the shape of the tail, which impedes their swimming. The colors of the Tosakin are similar to those of Ryūkins but they start to decolor later than do the Ryūkins. At times it takes three years before the color change starts.

(m) Long-finned Lionhead (Shūkin)—This is another fish which shows the skill of the master breeder, Kichigorō Akiyama. It was first produced in 1897 by crossing Ranchū and Oranda. Shūkins lack a dorsal fin, and might popularly be described as long-bodied, long-tailed Lionheads. In my own experiments I have been able to produce these fish by making crossings identical to those of Mr Akiyama, but have found that the percentage that these fish would breed true was only slightly over three per cent. The race of Shūkins did not last long. Today, the Shūkin and Shūkin-type fishes are either gone, or well on the road to extinction.

TOM CARAVAGLIA

A group of young Redcaps: called Tanchō in Japan or Hon Tou in China, where it originated. Because the concentration in this type is on head color pattern, less attention is paid to selection for type.

(n) Wakin-Lionhead Hybrid (Kinranshi)—This was produced by Mr Akiyama in 1902 from a crossing of the Lionhead with the Wakin. About one third of the offspring lack dorsal fins, and have the slimmer body of the Wakin. The Kinranshi did not have any great points of beauty or grace which would encourage breeders to perpetuate the race, and today it is considered an extinct variety.

(o) Iron-colored Ryūkin (Tetsuonaga)—Basically, Tetsuonaga are Ryūkins which have not gone through the decoloring phase by their second year. Tetsuonaga could probably be developed by selectively picking fish from Ryūkin broods which are late in decoloring, or fail to go through the decoloring phase at all. As Tetsuonaga go into their second year, their pectoral fins develop a yellowish metallic glint. Some American breeders of the Veiltail or Broadtail fish have strains which closely match the description of Tetsuonaga. Fish of this color are perpetuated by American breeders because they are quite hardy and often show a good fin development. Therefore, they are kept to be bred with more brightly colored fishes to maintain vigor and fin shape.

(p) Pompon (Hanafusa)—This fish has fleshy appendages growing from its nostrils like the Chinese Pompon or Narial Bouquet (Run chiu yü). They are different fish, however. The Chinese variety has a short, dorsal-less Lionhead type of body; the Japanese, which was thought to be extinct but rediscovered in 1950, is an Oranda type. The pompon itself is not as large in the Japanese variety.

World-wide

In recent years, these Japanese races have been sent to almost every country in the world where fishkeeping is a hobby, particularly the USA, England, Germany and France.

Many of these highly bred varieties are now being bred in and shipped from Hong Kong and Singapore, as well as Japan.

A cross between a Pearl Scale and a Broadtail showing some of the characteristics of both; for example the pearling along the abdomen and the broad tail. This is a male with well developed tubercles on the leading edge of the pectoral fins and on the gill covers.

NEAL TEITLER

American Goldfish

The two varieties of goldfish considered to have originated in the United States are the Comet Tail and the Veiltail.

The Legendary Veiltail

Veiltails have long fins, with little or no fork in the paired caudal fins. In the best specimens the ends of the long and graceful tail look as if they have been squared off with a knife, and indeed at some Veiltail competitions which were held in the United States in the early part of this century, exhibitors were accused of aiding nature in this respect.

Good Veiltails will also have extremely long anal fins, so in selecting young fish for potential future development, the length of the anal fins is an aid to predicting which of the youngsters are most likely to turn out to be particularly good.

Along with the squared-off caudal fins, the other characteristic giving Veiltails their distinctive beauty is the extremely high dorsal fin, which is matched by no other race of goldfish. Indeed, many long-tailed Fantails and Orandas are often called Veiltails, but if the high sail-like dorsal is lacking, these pretenders do not deserve the name.

As the Ranchū is the king of goldfish in Japan, the Veiltail is considered to be the premier fish in Western countries and is the symbol of excellence used by many aquarium societies.

Philadelphian Origin

Veiltails are thought to have originated in the Philadelphia area about the turn of the century as a mutant from the Ryūkin or Japanese Fantail. They immediately became popular and by crossing them with other fish—notably the Calico Telescope and the Black Moor—Veiltail strains of these two fishes were produced.

Veiltails are less hardy than the more common types of fish, and require rigid culling of the young to preserve the characeristics of square caudal and high dorsal fins. For these reasons, the strain has just about disappeared in the United States, with perhaps less than a dozen people successfully keeping and spawning these fish.

Commercial goldfish hatcheries in the United States have tried to raise Veiltails with no success, but descendants of fish exported from Philadelphia to Europe, notably England and Germany, are being raised successfully.

Veiltails today are probably not up to the standards of the original Philadelphia fish, nor is the proportion of long tails in each spawning as great. This may be due to injudicious crossings made in a misguided effort to improve the strain.

Comet Tail

Comet Tails, or Comets as they are usually known, are similar in body shape to the Shubunkin, although the standard calls for a longer and even thinner body than the wild fish. The tails of Comets should be as long as or longer than those of Shubunkins, and whereas the desired tail on the Shubunkin has rounded ends, on the Comet the ends should come to a point. Comets should be red or red and white.

Comets are one of the two varieties which originated in the USA, and they seem to have mutated from Ryūkins or red Fantails there. The Comets in Japan today come mainly from fish

A male Red-capped Veiltail. He has a good deep body, long tail and fins and a high, erect dorsal.   RICHARD LAW

of American origin. The author has produced Comet Tail fish by crossing female Ryūkins with male Crucian Carp.

Comets are one of the hardier and more active varieties and their constant swimming about gives us great pleasure. In America the Comet is the variety that is produced in the greatest number, millions being sold there every year, and very inexpensively. From the fact that they are so readily available, one can assume correctly that the Comet is a very hardy fish and they do well when left outdoors the year around.

Intense red, the nearer approaching scarlet the better, has always been the sought-after color for Comets, but the author has read that there is a yellow or canary-colored strain which is highly prized in England.

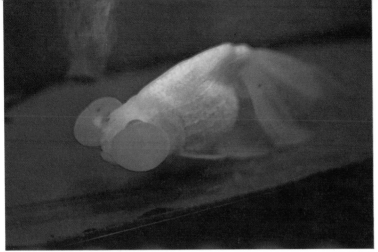

NEAL TEITLER

A Chinese bred Bubble-eye Goldfish with well-developed, deep orange bubbles or eye pouches. The far eye can be seen as just a black dot. The deformity at the base of the spine makes it undesirable as a breeder. The Chinese name for this fish is Shui Pao Yen.

V   Chinese Goldfish

Considering its long history of goldfishkeeping, and the active work that is being done today in producing new varieties, China truly deserves to be called the home of the goldfish. The respect that is given to the breeding of goldfish in China is shown by the issuance of many postage stamps depicting the high points in the art of goldfish breeding. There are stamps showing such fancy varieties as the Lionhead, crossbreed of Narial Bouquet and Outturned Operculum, Purple Oranda, Celestial, a goldfish with a bright red cap, etc.

China has produced the greatest number of goldfish races. Just how many depends on one's definition. Some varieties may be raised for only a few generations—not long enough to fix a standard. An almost limitless number of varieties can be turned out if all of the possible crosses and combinations of crosses are made, but this would serve no real purpose, since many of these theoretically possible types would offer nothing to those who appreciate the aesthetics of a beautiful fish. One could probably, with little difficulty, list over a hundred types of Chinese fishes, but for our purposes we will consider only the outstanding varieties.

Bubble-eye Goldfish. The calico color is unusual.

A Government Function

In China, full-time park officials are in charge of raising and managing goldfish in public ponds. It does not appear to be fashionable for goldfish to be kept privately these days. To see fine goldfish it is only necessary to go to one of the parks where they are displayed for the general public to enjoy; a family group quietly watching the exotic goldfish set out for the admiration of park visitors is a common sight in China. Often the fish are put out in ceramic bowls so that they can be observed at close range, and the finer points of the fish studied.

While the private breeder must make some compromise between what he would like to do and what necessity dictates, large ponds and other facilities are at the disposal of the park attendants. Further, the attendants who breed the fish in the public parks of China do not have the problems of the commercial breeder who must concentrate on developing the greatest number of saleable fish in the shortest time. The attendant working in the public park is only required to breed the best possible fish for the enjoyment of the public. The successful results obtained by the public goldfish breeders in China remind me of the work done in Japan on chrysanthemums in the Shinjuku Gardens, where full-time caretakers produce flowers of legendary beauty admired by all.

Many New Varieties

Many of the Chinese varieties of fish are so new that we cannot yet say whether they are firmly fixed as races, since when some of these newer types are bred, it is noticed that they do not always breed true. This makes us wonder if they will ever be perfected or if they will only be bred by selecting and re-selecting from many hybrid fish.

When classifying Chinese varieties, the features that give the fish their names are related to the particular development of the various body parts. The head, eyes, gill covers, nasal membranes, fins and scales are all considered when naming the fish. Most of the variations in the various body parts of Chinese fish can be found in one degree or another on the Japanese fish, but in addition there are some features that are peculiar to Chinese fish.

Head Types

There are six main types of head development that are named by the Chinese: high head, tiger head, goose head, lion head, toad head and rat head.

Eye Types

Seven main eye types are described. These are: common eyes;

A nacreous Pearl Scale Goldfish. RICHARD LAW

In older, simpler days, goldfish shows were not as elaborate as they are today. It was common practice to hold them in the garden of a leading fancier's home. This picture is about forty years old.

bubble eyes; tong pao yen—which are telescope eyes having the transparent cornea developed to an outstanding degree; upward-gazing or celestial eyes; pu tao yen—which are telescope eyes with dark purple eyeballs; chu sha yen or red eyes; and mandarin duck eyes, with one eye red and the other white.

Scale Types

Scale types found in Chinese fish include the common and transparent scales found in the Japanese fish, and in addition to these, there is the Chin choo yü or Pearl Scale.

Colors

Chinese fish show all the colors found in the Japanese varieties, and in addition there are two or three colors that are found only in Chinese fish. These colors are brown, blue and purple. We have talked about these colors before in describing Japanese fish, but only in connection with fish having transparent scales. In Chinese fish these colors appear on fish with non-transparent scales, which is what makes the coloration unique.

Purple is considered by some to be a new color, while others consider purple fish to be just better specimens of the brown goldfish selected for an intense purplish-brown cast. According to the latter, brown goldfish can be called purple, chocolate or bronze according to the intensity and shading of the pigment.

Blue goldfish are solid colored fish with a bluish-gray cast. The earlier blue fishes described all had telescope eyes, and it was thought by some that they might just be a subvariety or dilution of the Black Moor. The same conjecture was made about the brown fish since they were always depicted with telescope eyes; but it has been shown that both the brown and the blue fish can be raised with normal eyes, whereas the color of the Black Moor is genetically linked to the telescope eye characteristic.

There has also been a blue-brown goldfish developed, which has a body of blue with brown or bronze patches. The blue-brown goldfish was first mentioned by the well-known Chinese teacher, C. Chen, who did intensive research on the inheritance of the blue and brown factors in China in the early thirties.

The blue and brown colors are not the result of any decoloration but, as in the Calico or transparent-scaled fishes, these colors show on young fish as soon as the scales can be detected with the naked eye. However, both blue and brown goldfish can go through a decoloring phase, and in this respect their color seems to be unstable, as on many specimens of Black Moors which turn orange as they grow older.

A fairly common occurence in blue goldfish is a tendency to fade or turn light in color, as seen in this Chinese fish, the Chin Wen Yü. DR. SYLVAN COHEN

Mr Chen does not record any instances of his fish decoloring, and it may be that the instability of color in today's fish results from crosses made with other races of goldfish in order to produce new types. Examples of these new types are Blue Orandas and Brown Orandas. The resulting fish may inherit the tendency to decolor from their Oranda ancestors.

The decoloring of blue or brown fish is not always undesirable, as the decoloring of the fish can result in very attractive specimens. When blue fish completely decolor, they are all white, but as they are going through the decoloring phase they manifest for a time an attractive pattern of blue and white. The blue and white colors are distributed in much the same way as are the orange and black colors in Common Goldfish which are decoloring. On the decoloring blue fish, sometimes the color change does not go through to completion, and a permanently blue and white fish results.

Decoloring of brown fish or chocolate fish results in an orange-colored fish and, since there is nothing unique about an orange-colored fish, the changing of colors is considered undesirable.

Wild Colored Veiltail (Broadtail) male. This fish is more than a year old, but has not yet decolored, making it unlikely that he ever will. NEAL TEITLER

However, as on the blue fish, every so often the decoloring does not go through to completion, and this leaves the fish with a permanent color pattern that is unusual and attractive. This incomplete decoloration on brown fish with telescope eyes can result in fish with permanently colored brownish-black eyes on an orange body, and with a brownish-black back.

Decoloring of blue-brown goldfish can show two main color patterns. In one, the blue turns to white, leaving brown patches on a white background, and in the other, both the blue and the brown decolor, leaving a white fish with orange patches. The first can give fishes a striking beauty, but the latter change is considered undesirable, being neither a unique pattern nor especially attractive.

In China there is another general way of classifying goldfish, by the following names:

Wen shu (Japanese: Bun shu)—These include 20 varieties of the common type.

Ron shu (Japanese: Ryu shu)—These have protruding eyes, with about thirty types recognized.

Zokushu—There are about twenty types of these, characterized by the lack of a dorsal fin.

Having talked about the main features of Chinese goldfish and their classification, here are the names and a brief description of some of the main varieties.

Blue Goldfish (Lang Wen Yü)

The distinguishing characteristic of this fish is its color, bluish-purple. Early types of this fish seem to have had telescope eyes, but today they are found without telescope eyes and/or head growth, etc. As has been mentioned, the color is sometimes unstable.

Brown Fish, Chocolate Fish, Purple Fish (Tsu Yü)

The color is the distinguishing characteristic of this fish, and its variations and color phases have been described previously. As with the Blue, this seems to have been originally a telescope-eyed variety.

Calico colored Chinese Pompon with beautifully developed frills.

Pearl Scale (Chin Choo Yü)

The scales are hard and are raised in the center. There seem to be several color varieties of this fish, but the classic pattern is a basic red coloration with the raised center of each scale being white. Pearl Scales have a very short, barrel-shaped body. The fins are short and the caudal fin does not show any flecking, being square at the edges like the American variety of fish known as Broadtail.

Pompon, Narial Bouquet (Run Chiu Yü)

The distinguishing feature of this variety is the growth of the narial section or nostrils. These become large and ball shaped, and move about as the fish swims. An idea of how this looks might be gained from the name which is sometimes given to this fish in China: "Dragon playing with red velvet ball." The classic Chinese variety of this fish is usually considered to be one with no dorsal fin and with a short, Ranchū-like body.

Bubble-eye (Shui Pao Yen)

The distinguishing feature of this variety is the water-filled sac which protrudes under each eye. About fifteen years ago, fish imported from China had short, compact, Ranchū-like bodies, short fins and large but firm bubbles under each eye. Today the tendency for the Chinese breeders seems to be towards longer-tailed fish with even greater size to the water bubbles under the eyes, which are no longer firm, but bobble about somewhat as the fish swims. Whether of the new or older type, all Bubble-eyes should lack a dorsal fin completely and have a smooth back.

Toad Head (Hama Tou)

This fish seems to be derived from the same line as the Bubble-eye, but the head is broader and the body more rounded. The bubbles are not as well developed as on the Bubble-eye, but add to the broadness of the head, which is intended to resemble that of a toad. Again, this fish should have a smooth back without a dorsal fin.

A pair of Pompon Goldfish. This race is distinguished by the lack of a dorsal fin, the deep body, and particularly the development of the flesh appendages over the nostrils.

Redcap (Hon Tou)

These fish should be all white, except for the top of the head, which should be bright red. In the best varieties, the fish have a well-developed red hood. It seems to be a fairly new variety and there is great variation in body shapes, fin lengths and presence or absence of the dorsal fin, which seems to indicate that standards for the fish have not yet been fixed. There do not seem to be any reliable statistics as to the true breeding characteristics of the red head, and some breeders have been disappointed in getting too large a number of all-white fish from breedings of fish imported from China. In Japan this fish is known as Tanchō, which is the name of a Japanese crane that has a white body and a red crest.

Outturned Operculum (Fan Sai)

In this variety the gill covers fold back on themselves to expose the gill rakers to view. While some of the Fan sai are attractive fish in spite of the deformed gill covers, the peculiar development of the gill cover would seem to have limited appeal to fanciers. The outturned operculum seems to appear quite often among many varieties of goldfish, but usually it is considered to be a reason for discarding the fish, if not actually a sign of illness.

Chinese vs Japanese

If we compare the state of the goldfish breeder's art in Japan and China today, it seems that there are more varieties in China and the trend to develop new varieties continues there, while such work in Japan seems to be at a standstill. In order to get new varieties for the Japanese market, the Japanese goldfish supplier seems to be content with importing those that are developed in China. Chinese breeders will probably keep ahead in the development and sale of new varieties, if for no other reason than that they have access to the fishes which are developed in the public parks in China. If we consider the quality of the fishes raised in Japan with those of China, however, the picture is not all that bleak. While the economics of the Japanese market do not permit too much dabbling in new varieties, some of the older strains are being kept up very well. A good example of this is the high quality of the Japanese Ryūkins. Considered aesthetically, they are probably as fine as any fish ever bred, and continuing work and cooperation among the breeders of Japan goes on to keep up the quality of these fine fish and at the same time keep them inexpensive and available to all.

Chinese goldfish stamps. Left to right, top row: Hon Mao Tze (Oranda); Lan Lung Chin (Blue Demekin Telescope); San Jung Chin (hybrid of Pompon and Outturned Operculum). Second row: Tzu Mao Tzu (Pebble Oranda), Shui Pao Yen (Bubble-eye). Third row: Chin Choo Yü (Pearl Scale), Bu Tao Yen (Telescope Eyes with dark purple eyeballs), Tze Yu (Chocolate Oranda). Bottom row: Hon Tou (Redcap), Hei Pei Lung Ching (Black Dorsal Telescope).

An unusual, Pearl-colored Toad Head (Hama Tou). This fish is not an albino; the pupil has pigment. The bubbles are not as well developed as in the Bubble-eye. The foliage in the background is artificial. Abnormally developed fishes such as these are best kept indoors, or in a protected environment.

VI   The Environment

Certain species of fishes are physiologically capable of living only at low temperatures. These are true cold water fishes. Others, while able to exist and survive for periods of time at low temperatures—as during the winter—only thrive and increase in size at median temperatures. These latter are called warm water fish, and it is to this group that goldfish belong. Among aquarium hobbyists goldfish are sometimes thought of as cold water fish, but this is correct only when they are compared with the true tropical fish, which cannot survive low temperatures.

The Winter

In the autumn, as the days grow colder and the water approaches the 50°F range, the amount of food consumed is noticeably reduced. When the water temperature drops still lower, the fish may stop feeding altogether and go into hibernation on the bottom of the pond. It is safe to say that under the ice the fish require no food until spring, although under some circumstances goldfish will feed all winter. This can be proved by the number of goldfish that are caught on hook and line by those who go ice fishing. In spite of this, it is important to emphasize the fact that goldfish do not have to be fed during the winter and no attempt should be made to feed them, as uneaten food in the pond can pollute the water and kill the fish.

During the winter the fish do not move about much and their respiration rate is very low. The less they are disturbed the better, as activity consumes calories—calories that they will need in order to survive. Because of their reduced metabolism, they can pass the winter living off the nutritive elements that they store in their bodies throughout the warmer weather; it is likely that the major part of their winter reserve is built up in late September and October. At that time of year, food does not seem to be utilized so much to promote growth as to fatten them and carry them through the winter. In October, goldfish often seem to be in the best condition, and their bodies have a firm, full, robust appearance.

Freeze Over

So long as goldfish are fat and healthy, they do not seem to be uncomfortable when ice starts to cover the pond. Neither the cold of winter nor the thickness of the ice appears to affect them, if the fish themselves are not frozen. There are tales told of goldfish trapped in solid blocks of ice being revived completely when thawed out. It is difficult to see how this could happen, since the ice crystals would rupture the very cells of the fish. At any rate, if you value your fish, do not let them get completely frozen. Your local weather bureau will give you the maximum depth of frost for your area; be sure that your pond is at least twelve inches deeper to provide an ice-free area.

The ice should be broken at intervals to release the carbon dioxide and other gases that accumulate and become trapped beneath the ice. A stream of water from a gardenhose is very effective for melting the ice.

Living off their own bodies during the winter, goldfish can lose up to twelve per cent of their weight. As spring nears, the ice melts away, they start to move actively and come out of the deep parts of the pond into the shallows to feed. As the water reaches about 53°F, the goldfish start to swim around and with renewed feeding they increase in size, this growth continuing until the following autumn. Ice can reduce the light, and snow on ice can cut it off completely; therefore, only a minimum of plants should be allowed to remain over the winter. Otherwise, as the plants die and decay, they reduce the available oxygen.

The Summer

In the heat of summer, if the water temperature should reach 85°F or more, even a warm water fish like the goldfish will be distressed and there will be a drop in the rate of feeding. At such times, feeding has to be watched closely so that no excess amounts

Garden ponds can be either formal structures of brick, concrete or other building materials, or, as we see here, an almost natural body of water, heavily planted down to the banks.

of food are left to foul the water. Goldfish are most sensitive to bad water conditions at these high temperatures. A danger signal to watch for is the fish coming to the top of the water and gulping for air.

Not only uneaten food can foul the water in the dog days of summer; decaying leaves or algae can also, by their decomposition, reduce the amount of oxygen in the water. As the water temperature rises, the requirements for oxygen are at their highest, but increased temperatures reduce the capacity of the water to hold oxygen; a very precarious balance can result and the fishkeeper must be watchful.

Oxygen

If goldfish are to live and thrive, they must have an abundance of nourishing food and they must have suitable water in which to live. Goldfish are extremely tolerant of a wide range of water conditions, and they can live in either hard or soft, acid or alkaline water, but they do demand that the water have an adequate amount of dissolved oxygen. Whenever there is a decrease in the amount of oxygen in the water because of overcrowding, decomposition of the fishes' waste matter, decaying plants or algae or excess food putrefying, the fishes—as has been pointed out—will be in extreme danger.

Probably the safest way to protect the fish from suffocation due to lack of oxygen is to keep the aquarium clean and avoid over crowding and overfeeding. However, there is always the temptation to fill our containers to their capacity with fish and this must be guarded against. Fancy varieties seem to require more oxygen per inch of fish, and unfortunately they do not always warn us by looking distressed that their water is stifling them—they just die. A good rule is, therefore, the more valuable the fish, the more room it should be given to increase the safety margin.

A greatly overrated and dangerous method of keeping water oxygenated is to rely on the oxygen given off by green plants in the process of photosynthesis. Plants only give off oxygen in the presence of light, and at night the plants themselves respire and take the oxygen out of the water while giving off carbon dioxide. Algae, which are single-celled plants, go through the same cycle; that is, they release oxygen during photosynthesis and carbon

TOM CARAVAGLIA

A young male Pearl Scale Goldfish. Deep bodied, sluggish fishes like this one actually consume less oxygen in proportion to their body weight than do slimmer, more active fish.

dioxide in the dark. A crowded pond may show the fish at the top of the water at daybreak, gasping for air, waiting for the sunlight to reach the green plants so that they can start the oxygen-producing process. Even in the daytime, if the day is overcast, with low barometer readings, the presence of plants in the water may reduce the oxygen.

Almost any good thing can be carried too far, and an excess of oxygen can cause severe distress, particularly in long-finned fish. In a heavily planted pond or one which is dark green with algae, the oxygen production in bright sunlight can be so great that the normal balance of dissolved gases in the water is upset and gas bubbles will appear on the fins of the fishes, which can cause them to float at the surface and may make the fins split.

Deep Well Water

Water from deep wells is usually deficient in oxygen and may contain gases such as carbon dioxide and methane which are toxic to fish. Such water should be boiled and aerated very heavily for several days before use.

In nature, most species of fish will move about freely from the shallows to the depths and back again, searching out the areas which are most comfortable to them with regard to temperature and dissolved oxygen in the water. Because of this instinct, they are able to escape harmful surroundings. In a shallow garden pond or an aquarium, goldfish have no way to escape extremes of temperature or poorly oxygenated water, so they are at the mercy of their keepers.

To protect against oxygen content fluctuation, it is helpful to have some way to circulate the water and to set up a splashing action. A waterfall or a fountain is a good way to get the water splashed and aerated, so that these serve a very useful as well as decorative function. An air pump, like those used in indoor aquaria, can also be helpful. This would not have to be run constantly, but only when fish show signs of distress, or perhaps as a precaution in very hot weather.

Water Temperatures

Goldfish are poikilothermic; that is, they do not maintain a constant body temperature as do warm-blooded animals. The temperature of the goldfish will vary with the temperature of the water. Under natural conditions where changes of water temperature are more or less gradual, goldfish can adjust to relatively great extremes of temperature. On the other hand, sudden temperature changes can be fatal. When goldfish are put into water with a $10°F$ temperature difference from the water from which they were taken, they need about an hour to get fully adjusted to the new temperature. They may show their distress by being sluggish, lying on the bottom or perhaps on their sides. If they are shifted several times in a short period of time between waters with a 10°F temperature difference, the fish will soon become unconscious, and in most cases they die. Sometimes goldfish are put into cold water such as might be found in a well, and they start to swim about with great vigor. It might seem that they are invigorated by the bracing water, but the truth is that it is because of their agony that they are so active.

Temperature and Breeding

Later on, when we discuss breeding in detail, the ways to make

This is a so-called "scaleless" Fantail, known in England as a "matt." Actually, the scales are present but they are transparent. The pearl-like tubercles forming on his gill covers show that this is a male in breeding condition.

use of temperature cycles to stimulate spawning will be covered, but it can be said here that some seasonal temperature variations throughout the year seem to be necessary if a goldfish is to develop fully. When goldfish are kept under constant high temperatures, such as are maintained in a tropical fish aquarium, they will grow extremely fast and may have exceptionally fine fin development; but tropical conditions are not natural to goldfish and those raised under them seldom develop any vivid colors and are generally quite delicate, with a reduced resistance to disease. A further drawback is that goldfish raised under a constant high temperature are very often found to be sterile.

It is a great mistake to treat goldfish with extreme physical developments like the Lionhead and Veiltail as semi-tropical fishes. Failure to subject these to cold hibernation conditions has resulted in strains which are delicate in health, and this results eventually in weak progeny.

Chemicals

In the typhoon which hit the city of Ise, goldfish from the Yatomi district were washed away and carried down to brackish waters, where they survived; this indicates that goldfish are extremely tolerant of the salt content in water. However, they must be protected against certain chemicals which man can introduce into the water supply. Today, most places treat drinking water with chemicals before it is sent through the mains. Chlorine is the chemical most frequently used for water purification; indeed, at times when water is freshly drawn from the tap a strong odor of chlorine can be detected. At this concentration chlorine is not harmful to humans, but it can be fatal to goldfish.

Fluorine, which is put into drinking water to combat tooth decay, does not seem to affect fishes.

Sunlight

Since goldfish live under the water, it might be thought that it is not necessary for them to get any sunlight, but some is indispensable if the fish are to develop properly. When goldfish are kept outdoors in a sunny location, they begin to feed earlier in the spring and will feed later on into the fall than they would if they were in a shaded pond. With the increased feeding, the fish will, as expected, grow big and strong and the sun also improves the color of the fish. They start their decoloring phase earlier and their final colors are more beautiful. However, in a plantless pond made of uncolored concrete, the effect of sunlight on the matt and nacreous groups is to bleach out the colors. The black and blue (which is also really black) pigments disappear, while the red and yellow pigments concentrate into small areas, usually towards the head, leaving the fish pale and colorless. The metallic groups lose the black pigment cells and only the red and orange cells will survive, but in a more intense pigmentation.

But if the pond is densely packed with thriving plants of the free-growing kind, such as Hornwort or *Elodea densa*, all three scale groups seem to benefit, and as noted, all colors become more intense. While plants are not indispensable to successful goldfish-keeping, it must be acknowledged that active plant growth, particularly in dense masses, preserves and enriches the coloring. This automatically calls for a cautionary word: in Britain, at least, sunshine is not something taken for granted, and fishpond keepers are forced to live on a razor's edge during the short summers lest two or more consecutive dull days should wipe out the fishes in a heavily planted pond. One insurance against such an eventuality is to keep a circulating water pump going 24 hours a day. Not only will the pump maintain a reasonable level of oxygen in the water, but it will also prevent it from becoming too warm, especially if the water is returned to the pond in a spray.

If an aquarium or bowl is set in a sunny window, however, be careful that it does not become too hot. Small bodies of water heat more rapidly than do large ones.

Other Factors

There are, obviously, other factors besides sunlight which affect the color of goldfish. Since here we are mainly concerned with environment, we will not at this point consider the effect of heredity on the coloring of the fish. Water temperatures, water depth, material dissolved and suspended in the water, the type of pond bottom and the fish's diet all have an influence on color. These factors also have a profound effect on the size and shape of the fish, as well as determining in some instances the ratio between

In China, goldfish are raised in a parklike atmosphere by public attendants whose lives are devoted to the fishes' care and breeding.

the body and fin lengths on the fish. It is possible to distribute the fry from a single spawning among a dozen ponds, each with different environmental conditions, and on examining them at the end of the year it would be hard to believe that the fish are all full brothers and sisters. All of the fish could be in good health, so that the differences in colors and shapes cannot be explained on the basis of a lack of some feature essential to the fish's development in any one of the ponds. An environment which gives goldfish their greatest growth while maintaining their health might be considered to be the best one from a purely biological viewpoint. If this environment should hinder the development of an essential feature for a particular type, it would not be a good environment from the viewpoint of the goldfish fancier. An example of this is seen when Ranchūs or Lionheads are placed in very large ponds. The fish tend to get longer and more slender in the body than is desired, and the head does not develop well. Orandas, which should have long tail fins, sometimes do not develop these when the fish are placed in too large a pond—all of the growth goes into the body. Here it might be pointed out that those fish which grow to great size might conceivably still develop into superior specimens after two or three years when they have reached their full growth in body length, but unfortunately there is not enough evidence on this point.

In summing up, it can be said that after one has provided an environment to assure healthy fish, other factors have to be considered individually to determine whether an environment is a good one from a fancier's viewpoint, particularly when he is striving to develop a particular feature in his strain of fish.

The English are noted for their formal plantings, and their formal goldfish aquariums are not far behind. Here in an elegant setting we see a charming group of Veiltails (Broadtails) and Shubunkins.

VII   Goldfish Indoors

The best place to raise goldfish would be in large ponds or in a natural swamp, but since not many of us have these at our disposal, we have to decide whether we will raise our fishes outdoors in pools or indoors in tubs or tanks of one type or another. Whichever method we use is largely determined by our circumstances.

Advantages

Keeping goldfish indoors in tanks gives us a better chance to view them, both from the top and from the side. They cannot hide beneath a lily pad or sink to the bottom of a pond just when we wish to show them off.

Another advantage to having our fish in tanks, particularly glass ones, is that we can more readily spot the start of trouble and take steps to correct it.

Against these, one must consider the drawbacks. For example, fish that spend their entire life outdoors generally have brighter colors than those which are kept inside. In addition, there is the loss of the natural food which continually falls into the outdoor pool. Seasonal variations of light and temperature are not nearly so pronounced indoors, and while this is not always completely desirable, the fact is that fish which are subjected to seasonal changes of temperature and light seem to be hardier and stronger.

By far the greatest difficulties encountered when keeping goldfish indoors are usually related to the crowding which they frequently are forced to endure. Because of its limited volume, the quality of the water in tanks is subject to more rapid changes in chemical content and pH value. There is the common tendency to overcrowd the tank, which causes losses, and overfeeding too is a critical problem, because in a limited space even a relatively small amount of uneaten food can foul the water.

How many tanks and what size tanks are needed for the proper care of goldfish? More than one is desirable, and tanks should be of the 20- to 30-gallon size, if possible. However, if space or other considerations make more than one tank impractical, a single tank will do—one of at least 20 gallons, if possible.

Bowls

In the early days, small bowl-shaped glass basins were often seen hanging in front of Japanese houses. These were suspended in a net of rough mesh. Another picturesque aquarium was a small circular glass basin, the rim of which was shaped like the fronds of a plant waving in the water. While these and other all-glass aquariums sold today for goldfish are decorative, their shape distorts the fine points of the goldfish. Because of this image-distorting effect, they are not the ideal choice, but if one must use

The size and shape of goldfish containers are limited only by the imagination.

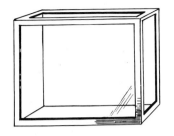 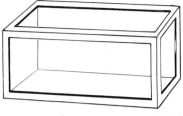

(Left) A tall narrow tank will support fewer fishes than will a long low one (right) even though both contain the same amount of water.

them, care should be taken to present the maximum amount of water surface to the air. If the bowl narrows at the top, fill it only to its widest part. The point to remember, regardless of the type of aquarium we use, is that the amount of fish it can hold without artificial aeration is a direct function of the area of the water surface as related to its depth. A tall narrow aquarium will support fewer fishes than a broad shallow aquarium of the same gallon capacity. Increasing the height of an aquarium without proportionately increasing the other dimensions will not only not increase the fish capacity, it may even decrease it.

Selecting Your Goldfish

The usual source for a beginner is a pet shop or pet department in a variety or department store. Most of these carry three to five of the commoner varieties in an assortment of sizes. Only the larger shops and departments stock the fancier varieties, such as the Oranda, Lionhead, Pearl Scale and Bubble-eye.

For the beginner, it might be just as well to start with the less expensive, hardier varieties.

The advanced hobbyist or more ambitious beginner should contact a goldfish society for information and sources (see Appendix).

Fish which are being acquired for aquarium keeping are usually immature specimens, and it is difficult to determine the finer points which will only become evident as the fish mature. But regardless of the source, there are certain things which should be observed: the water in the tank where the fish are kept should be clear; the fish should not be overcrowded; there should be no dead fish floating in the tank; the fishes' fins (particularly the dorsal) should be erect and the tail fanned out; the fish should not be gasping at the top for air, nor should they be clustered in one corner under a faucet; their color should be bright and the fish active. Examine each fish carefully; it should be free of marks, torn fins or blemishes, and the bottom line should be gently convex starting at the gills. A flat or concave stomach indicates that the fish has not been fed properly or has been otherwise adversely affected. Thin fish should be avoided. This is not to confuse a naturally slim fish like the Comet with an unhealthy one, because even the Comet will have a noticeably rounded stomach.

Taking Them Home

At one time goldfish were transported in small wax cartons, but these are a thing of the past. Today, they are placed in plastic bags, which are then sealed to prevent leakage during transport. Some of the more advanced stores will even pump oxygen into the bag.

Avoid keeping the fish in the bags any longer than necessary, and also be careful of extremes of temperature on the way home, particularly on a very hot or very cold day.

At one time, hobbyists were instructed to "float" the bags in the tank to equalize the temperature. Today, we know that because the microscopic pores in the bag permit gas exchanges, this practice is harmful. Either pour the fish, with their own water, into a glass or enamel container which can be floated to equalize the temperature or, if there is very little difference between the bag temperature and the aquarium temperature, the new fish can be introduced directly into the tank.

If you are sure that the water in which the goldfish were carried is disease-free, just submerge and tip the container so the fish swims out; if you are in doubt as to the quality of the water, net the fish and gently lower the net into the water, then allow the fish to swim out. Never flip or drop a fish onto the surface of the water.

Quarantine

Quarantining new fish for ten days to two weeks is highly

A Pearl-colored Oranda in an aquarium decorated with artificial plants.

recommended. While it is unlikely that your fish is carrying any disease if you have selected carefully from a reliable source, it is always possible that it may be incubating an ailment. Even the most experienced of fishkeepers cannot spot problems in the very early stages.

A quarantine aquarium or hospital tank can be any small aquarium or large bowl. It should be completely unfurnished, but an air stone should be provided if at all possible.

If the fish shows no sign of ill health during the quarantine period, it can be released into the main aquarium.

Tanks

Today, most aquariums are rectangular with glass panes set in a stainless steel frame. An aquarium of 20-gallon capacity is the smallest that should be considered for goldfish, and one of 30 gallons is perhaps the ideal choice, although it must be admitted that many people have kept, and enjoyed, one or two fish for many years in a small aquarium or bowl. Larger aquariums are somewhat inconvenient, since they are not easily moved by one person, nor is it always easy to find the proper place for an over-sized aquarium.

Because of its lack of distortion, the flat-sided aquarium is the best shape for appreciating the splendor of our fish. Even in this type of aquarium, we do have the problem of a film forming on the inside of the tank after a while, although we may have an air pump and a filter going constantly. This film will be either gray or green, depending upon the amount of light that reaches the tank. Because it obscures our view as well as being unsightly, there is a tendency among hobbyists to scrape this film off as fast as it accumulates, but it should be borne in mind that the film does serve a beneficial purpose. Since the film is made up of living single-celled plants, it will release some oxygen into the water; even more important, the film helps to purify the water by digesting some of the harmful waste matter and breaking it down into more innocuous compounds. Because the film does serve these purposes, it is a good idea to keep just the front pane scraped clean.

Ornaments

Various ornamental objects are often placed in tropical fish aquariums. For some species of tropical fish these ornaments also serve a useful purpose because the fish can lay their eggs in the crevices and recesses, and the fry can also utilize them for shelter. Although I personally think that artificial ornaments add nothing to a goldfish aquarium and even tend to detract from the fish, ornaments are a matter of taste. After all, goldfish are kept for the pleasure they give, and if ornaments please you, by all means use them. Just be sure that they were manufactured for aquarium use, otherwise they may have toxic or otherwise undesirable properties.

Ornamental colored gravel is sometimes advocated as a bottom covering for the aquarium but gravel can cause problems in keeping the aquarium clean. When uneaten food and waste matter get down into the gravel, a foul decomposition starts to take place which spoils the water and robs it of oxygen. The major justification for having gravel in an aquarium is for the rooting of plants, but this can also be done in small pots. Many plants suitable for the aquarium do not have to be rooted anyway. But if a landscaped tank appeals to you, gravel must be used. To keep it clean, stir the gravel occasionally with a stick about $\frac{1}{2}$-inch in diameter. Allow the stirred-up material to settle and then siphon off the mulm. Replace with fresh, aged or dechlorinated water.

Water Quality

A key point in raising goldfish at home, and also in fish farming, is to make sure that the water conforms to the fish's natural requirements. Fortunately, goldfish seem to be able to tolerate—within reason—just about any kind of water, and only badly deteriorated water harms them. Goldfish can live in soft or hard water, acid or alkaline water; they are even found in brackish waters. This does not mean that they will do well in these waters. It has been noted that the water in ponds which provide optimum conditions result in more rapid growth and more vivid colors.

However, since no definitive answers are available as to which type of water would be best for goldfish, the best we can do is to list the harmful factors, and since there are variables other than water quality, it will take further research before anyone can say which is the one best type of water. Without vouching for its authority, we must mention that some breeders feel that soft water of almost neutral pH is necessary for raising the extremely delicate Veiltail goldfishes.

Absolutely soft water, such as rain or distilled water, will not support goldfish; a small amount of hardness is required.

Temperature

While goldfish are quite tolerant of temperature extremes (from just above freezing to about 85°F), they do not appreciate sudden or extreme changes. The preferred temperature is between 65° and 70°F. Never drop goldfish suddenly into water which is more than two or three degrees different from their own. If you cannot adjust the temperature of the new water, put the goldfish into a container with some of the water to which he is accustomed and

This German bred fish, like the Japanese Watonai, is a hybrid of the Wakin and Ryūkin.

allow it to float in the new water until the temperature has equalized. Fish are capable of detecting temperature changes of as little as 0.04 per cent.

Chlorine

Water as it comes from the tap these days is often heavily chlorinated. At times, the concentration of chlorine will be so great that it can be smelled when the tap is opened. Chlorine in heavy concentration can kill goldfish, but if chlorinated water is exposed to the air for two or three days, the chlorine will be entirely dissipated or reduced to a harmless level; if the water is aerated while it is being matured, the dissipation of the chlorine will be much faster and if one does not have the time to wait for the natural dissipation, the water may be agitated or splash-poured back and forth between two buckets. The chlorine in water can also be neutralized chemically; preparations for this are sold in pet stores. One of the chemicals used for the reduction or removal of chlorine is sodium thiosulfate, at a dosage of one grain per gallon of water, or photographer's hypo, one tablespoon to about forty gallons of water.

Other methods of removing chlorine from water are by heating it to 180°F for a half hour or more; using one of the special charcoal filters which are available for the removal of chlorine; or using water from the hot water tap, drawn hot and cooled to the proper temperature. For the hobbyist, the most practical of methods seems to be the combination of aging and aeration, and this is even more effective if the water is exposed to sunlight.

Hardness

The "hardness" of water is a measure of the amount of calcium or magnesium compounds dissolved in the water. It is usually expressed as grains of calcium carbonate and may be measured as "parts per million" (ppm) or "degrees of hardness" (dH). One dH = 17.1 ppm. A dH between 50 and 200 is satisfactory.

Hard water can be softened by diluting it with distilled water or clean rainwater. Ion exchange resins, available commercially, will remove the calcium and magnesium ions which cause the hardness, replacing them with soft sodium ions.

Fluorescent tubes which bring out the red and gold of a fish have been developed. They are marketed under such trade names as "Gro-Lux." The natural red of this group of Comets has been heightened and intensified by being photographed under this type of bulb.

Kits to test the degree of hardness are also available. It is best to test the water before attempting to alter its hardness.

pH

This is a measure of acidity or alkalinity of the water. To check the pH, a measured amount of water is put into a test vial, a drop or two of indicator solution added, and the resulting color change is read against a color chart which is usually calibrated above or below these readings. 7.0 is neutral; readings below that are acid and above, alkaline.

Tiny amounts of sodium biphosphate or dilute tannic acid may be added to make the water more acid, while sodium bicarbonate will add alkalinity. All changes must be gradual, with a fresh reading taken after each addition of chemical. Add some ground oyster shell or coarse ground agricultural limestone to the filter material if the tank has a tendency to turn acid continually.

No doubt tropical fishes are very susceptible to the pH, but not so much the goldfish. At 6.4 (acid), the colors are at the brightest, and 8.4 (highly alkaline), the dullest. A water on the acid side seems to reduce the outer mucus covering to a minimum, and when held in the hand the fish feels rough. Alkaline water encourages the development of mucus, and the fish has a slimy, slippery feel to it. A favorite trick with British breeders, when entering a competitive show, is to transfer the fish into a tank with a slightly acid pH a week or so before the event. This is done to bring out the colors better. A quicker method is immersion in a mild table salt solution which has the same effect of thinning out the mucous covering; but remember, the mucous covering is the defense of the fish against contagion—remove it and infection becomes a possibility.

The Balanced Aquarium

When it was discovered that plants give off oxygen during photosynthesis, the theory of the balanced aquarium became popular. Briefly, this stated that since fish take in oxygen and give off carbon dioxide while plants do the opposite, it should be possible to set up a situation in which the natural functions of the plants and fish support each other.

This never quite worked out, however. Plants respire, or breathe, the same way as animals do, and during this process take in oxygen and release carbon dioxide. While it is true that during photosynthesis the amount of oxygen liberated is greater than the amount absorbed by respiration, and in a thriving, well-lit aquarium bubbles may be seen arising from the plants, nevertheless the ability of aquarium water to absorb oxygen is limited and the surplus passes off at the surface. When the light is withdrawn, the plants consume the oxygen dissolved in the water until such time as the returning light starts the process again.

It was noticed that in many of the so-called "balanced aquariums" fish would be gasping at the water surface early in the morning, but as the daylight reached the plants the fish would leave the water surface and not show any signs of oxygen lack.

In a sense, an aquarium could be balanced so that the fish would survive without any outside source of air from air pumps or water circulators, but this can occur only when the water surface is adequate to carry the fish over those periods when the plants are not generating any oxygen. If we stop to think about it for a minute, what this really means is that this surface must be capable of supporting the fishes' oxygen requirements whether or not any plants are present, and that the plants are useful for maintaining the quality of the water rather than for oxygenating it. Plants also reduce the possibility of water turning green by competing with the algae for nutrients.

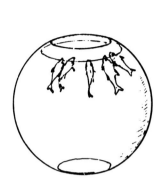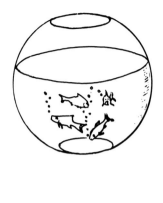

When fishes "hang" at the surface something is wrong. Check to see if there are too many for the size of the container or if overfeeding has polluted the water. Bowls shaped like these should be filled to the widest point (right—correct), not to the top (left—incorrect).

Air Surface

The air surface is far more important than the total volume of water, although both are factors in determining the number of fish which an aquarium can safely maintain. For example, a tall narrow aquarium can hold fewer fish—all other factors being equal—than can the same amount of water in a low, wide aquarium.

We must also remember that the larger the fish, the greater the quantity of oxygen required. One two-inch fish requires about fifty per cent more oxygen (and gives off a proportionately greater amount of carbon dioxide) than two one-inch fish. This is because the dimensions increase arithmetically while bulk increases geometrically.

Algae

All growing plants serve a useful function in the aquarium, including the single-celled algae which give us our green water. Green algae, however, are subject to rapid growth when conditions are right and a population explosion of algae can give rise to troubles, perhaps a killing-off of fish if care is not exercised. To avoid this, we must never let the water become too dark a green.

As a rule of thumb, an experienced aquarist judges water quality by its color, which should be light green. But it should not be so green that we cannot make out our fishes clearly, since we are then arriving at the danger point of too much algae in the water.

It might seem paradoxical that a growth of plant life can be harmful, but even under natural conditions large numbers of fish have been killed off when nature goes awry. Large numbers of Gray Mullet and Sea Bass frequently die off when they swim into narrow-mouthed inlets in sufficient numbers to use up the oxygen supply. In addition, we all can recall stories of the infamous red tide which kills off large numbers of fish and shellfish. The red tide is made up of minute single-celled organisms which, for some unexplained reasons, at times have a tremendous population explosion. Again, in nature, there are cases of winter deaths where large numbers of fish die for lack of oxygen because the surface ice becomes so thick that it cuts off the surface oxygen and also prevents the plants from carrying out photosynthesis.

Control of algae is not usually too difficult, if we reduce the two factors which cause its proliferation—that is, excess light and excess decomposing organic matter in the water. Like death and taxes, algae will always be with us. The spores can be introduced with water, with fresh plants, with live food and many other ways. Some algae can enter into a dry spore form which can be airborne and which will regenerate when immersed in water.

So the problem then is one of controlling, rather than eliminating, the problem. Some light is necessary to maintain plant growth. By experimenting you can determine how much and what strength will support the higher plants, while keeping the algae growth to a minimum.

The other factor, decomposing matter, can be controlled by proper feeding and siphoning the bottom regularly to pick up settled humus.

Aquarium Plants

Plants in an aquarium serve both a useful and ornamental purpose, but we are limited to those which can be used with goldfish, who enjoy eating the more tender plants. Several varieties of *Vallisneria*, Anacharis and the various *Cryptocorynes* are all good plants for the aquarium and are not usually nibbled. *Cabomba* and

Myriophyllum are often available in pet stores, but these will soon be eaten by goldfish unless the fish are few in number and they are fed heavily.

Because goldfish do eat live plants, many people have turned to using artificial ones. The same could be said of these as of other ornaments. They are not functional, but they certainly are decorative. If a jungle of colorful plastic fronds pleases you, there is no harm done. Plastic plants have a further advantage; they can be removed and scrubbed—warm water and a clean brush only, please; no soap or detergents. Some people compromise by combining artificial with natural plants to create a pleasing as well as practical effect.

In outdoor pools, Water lilies, whose leaves float on top of the water, are beneficial in that they condition and oxygenate the water; but Water lilies do have one drawback: fish have a tendency to hide under the pads and consequently they do not become accustomed to people. The same disadvantages can occur in home aquariums if they are too heavily planted; the fish will tend to hide and not show themselves off as much as we would like.

Another drawback to having too many plants in an aquarium is that we may not always notice our fish making spawning attempts or we may not notice their eggs in the dense plant growth.

Aged Water

The tank should, if possible, be refilled with water which has been aged in a glass, plastic or enamel container. If aged water is not available, tap water of the proper temperature may be used after certain precautions have been observed: run the water at least fifteen minutes before using any, in order to eliminate any copper which may have accumulated from the pipes. Check the pH, and if it is acid (below 7.0) add a pinch of bicarbonate of soda, enough to bring the pH to 7.0. A teaspoon of aquarium salt should be added to each bucket of water. However, the addition of salt is to be made only when siphoned water is being replaced—never add salt when merely replacing water which has evaporated. Also add one of the commercially available chlorine neutralizers, in the quantities indicated on the label.

Changing Water

Filters and air pumps reduce the frequency with which we have to change the water, and also permit us to make these water changes at our convenience.

At one time it was felt that the older water was, the better. Today we know that this is not so. Aquarium experts advise us to change at least ten per cent of the water about once a week, even if the tank seems to be in good order. If the tank is in poor condition, that is if the water is turbid, or the fishes are hanging at the surface, if they are pinch-bellied or lying on the bottom, a change of one third to one half is indicated.

Using a siphon hose, siphon the water from the bottom areas, picking up as much detritus and mulm as possible in the process. If the gravel is stirred lightly and allowed to settle before siphoning, you will be able to remove that much more waste matter. After the tank has settled again, you can resiphon to remove any additional material.

Use Buckets

Should it be necessary to change the entire aquarium, a different procedure must be observed. Half-fill a plastic or enamel bucket with water from the aquarium and place your fish in this. If you have a great many fish, use several buckets. In order to prevent the fish from suffocating in their cramped quarters, drop an air stone into each bucket and make sure that it is bubbling. Siphon as much water as possible from the bottom of the tank and pick up as much mulm as possible in the process. If the gravel is polluted, as evidenced by blackening and foul odor, it should be discarded and replaced with fresh. Washing polluted gravel is not sufficient to cleanse it; it must be air- and sun-dried, a process which—considering the low cost of aquarium gravel—is hardly worthwhile.

The newer gravel should be thoroughly washed, spread over the bottom with the front and center part lower than the back and sides, and covered with brown paper. The water is poured onto this until the aquarium is three-quarters full, when the paper should be removed. Plants and ornaments can be placed in it at this stage and the balance filled. If you have used aged water, you can put the bucket with the fish in it in the aquarium, tip it over and allow them to swim out, but be careful that you don't cause an overflow. If enough aged water is not available, then use the bicarbonate, salt and chlorine neutralizer. However, it is not necessary to add them to each bucket. They can all be added at once, after the aquarium is filled, but before the fishes are put in. If possible, allow the aquarium water to age 24 to 48 hours before returning the fishes.

Don't Crowd

The fewer fish in the tank and the less they are fed, the longer the interval between changes—but don't starve your fish either.

Some people, in order to accelerate the growth of their fish, keep them in bare aquariums with strong aeration and feed them frequently—several times a day. Undoubtedly this does hasten their growth, but fish kept in this manner will require frequent water changes, and it is a method hardly recommended for the aquarium in the living room, as it is rather unsightly.

On the other hand, if you just want to keep an aquarium of beautiful goldfish, you can feed them two or three times a week, have strong filtration and aeration and enough light to keep your plants in good condition, and it will seldom be necessary to make water changes.

Pump and Filter

Thanks to such aids as the air pump and the filter, life has been made easier both for us and for the fish. Filters will remove uneaten food and other solid wastes, while the circulation of the water will help maintain the proper oxygen level. Air pumps send their streams of bubbles into the water to oxygenate it further. The bubbles streaming up through the water do, to a degree, help transfer oxygen to it, but it appears that the main value of the air stream is to agitate the water surface. This agitation greatly increases the surface area in contact with the air, and thus the interchange of carbon dioxide into the air and oxygen into the water is greatly accelerated.

The movement of the water by the filter and air stream greatly increases the activity of the fish. Fish in oxygenated water show a better appetite and, with the increased feeding and activity, their growth is much greater than would normally be expected in a small indoor aquarium. There is some question as to whether the increased growth of fish by means of this heavy aeration is entirely desirable, because the fish may become dependent upon heavy aeration. Some feel that the forced growth leads to very delicate fish and often sterile ones. Still, taking these possibilities into account, aeration has proved its value in the overwhelming majority of cases; in fact, the indoor goldfish aquarium would not be as popular and practical as it is today were we to be deprived of the benefits of aeration and filtration.

Types of Filters

Aquarium filters may be divided into three categories:

Undergravel filters: These are perforated plastic plates which are placed on the bottom of the aquarium and then covered with gravel. Air tubes at each end cause a circulation of the aquarium water through the gravel and up again through the tubes. The bacteria in the gravel act to purify the water as it passes through. These are extremely effective in tropical fish aquariums. They may be used in goldfish aquariums also if there are not too many inhabitants, but the action is not rapid enough to remove all the waste matter produced when an aquarium is substantially crowded. Of course, ideally an aquarium should never be crowded, but it does happen.

Outside filters: These are plastic boxes containing a bed of activated bone charcoal or carbon covered with either fiberglass or absorbent cotton-like synthetic material, usually Dacron or nylon. A siphon tube takes the water from the aquarium, and passes it through filter material into a chamber for clear water. From there an air lift tube connected to the air pump returns the purified water to the aquarium, completing the circulation. In addition to the inexpensive outside filters which are powered by an air pump, there are larger versions of the outside filter which have a water pump incorporated into their design. These are somewhat more expensive, but they do provide a greater filtering capacity and a more rapid circulation of the water, and are recommended for larger and more crowded aquariums.

Bottom filters: Simplest to operate and least expensive of all, these consist basically of a plastic box containing charcoal and glass wool. This box is placed at the bottom of the aquarium, usually in a corner where it is inconspicuous. An air tube circulates the water through the charcoal and glass wool.

Both of the latter two types must be cleaned, the frequency depending upon the number of fish kept. A good rule of thumb is a minor cleaning once a week and a major cleaning at least once a month. For a minor cleaning, just disconnect the filter box and the air tube, rinse the fiber and back-flush the filter to remove the larger particles of dirt from the charcoal; then it can be placed back in use. For a major cleaning, the fiber should be replaced and the charcoal first rinsed and then baked in an oven for ten minutes at 400°F. Replace the charcoal every six months. Filter brushes are available which will clean the tubes, and the filter box itself should be cleaned like any other piece of plastic. Use water only, never chemicals, when cleaning filters.

Filters are particularly valuable during the summer months, when, due to the higher temperatures, a fish's metabolism increases. At this time they breathe faster, eat more and of course the waste products of metabolism increase proportionately. In addition, the breakdown of organic matter in the aquarium is more rapid. If your tank is either near or above capacity, it is particularly important to reduce the number of fish during the warmer months. Some of the signs that toxins are accumulating in the aquarium are milky water, bubbles forming and floating on the surface, fish gulping air at the surface, slick coating on the surface of the aquarium glass and fish "piling up" in the corners.

Heaters

We have mentioned the use of air pumps and filters as important aids to goldfishkeeping. You might also want to consider an electric heater equipped with a thermostat. Because goldfish come from a temperate climate, where the temperature can and does vary widely, it is obvious that the heater is not nearly as necessary for goldfish as it is for tropical fish which are adapted to a limited high temperature range. As a matter of fact, an inexpensive device to lower water temperature during the heat of the summer might be more useful to goldfishkeepers than would be a heater. Perhaps some day someone will develop and market a water cooler inexpensive enough for the hobbyist.

In spite of this, a heater can still be put to good use. Heaters set to go on at a temperature of 45°F can be used to prevent tanks from freezing in an unheated fishhouse. Also, if the water is kept at 45°F or higher throughout the winter, the fish will not become sluggish and will continue to feed. The benefits will be evident in the spring in the form of more vigorous fish.

Another use for heaters is to induce the goldfish to spawn early in the year when the water temperatures have not yet reached the level at which goldfish will naturally spawn. In the Tōhoku district in the northeastern part of Japan, some breeders use electric heaters to get their fish to spawn in March or April. In the Tokyo-Yokohama area, encouraging earlier spawnings by the use of electric heaters has not been found necessary, since the temperatures in that area start the fish spawning early enough to give adequate growth for commercial purposes.

Some fanciers keep a low-wattage, sealed heater just below the surface of their garden ponds to keep an area ice-free all winter. This prevents the buildup of gas which sometimes takes place in ice-sealed ponds.

Although air pumps, filters and heaters can add to our convenience in keeping goldfish, we can do without them if we pay attention to the following precautions: avoid overcrowding the aquarium; feed and change water with care; and exercise care in the selection of varieties and sizes of fishes placed together.

If our aquarium is intended solely as a showpiece or a vessel in which to view and admire our fish, our aquarium setup indoors can be a simple one.

Fish Size

In selecting fish for our aquarium, it is well to remember that the larger fish will get more than their share of the food and that they may annoy smaller fishes by nipping at their fins. If the disparity in size is too great, they may even swallow them. Also, the relatively slow-swimming varieties, such as Lionheads, Orandas, Celestials, etc., cannot compete with the more active types such as Shubunkins and Comets. In a tank of mixed varieties, there is always a tendency for one or two fish to bully the others, so if space and inclination permit, it is a good idea to keep fish of the same variety and size in a tank.

Tubificid worms, commonly known as *Tubifex*, are used extensively for feeding tropical fishes as well as goldfish. This freshwater Puffer is feasting on a small colony of *Tubifex* that has established itself in the aquarium gravel.

VIII   Food and Feeding

In Japan at one time silkworm chrysalides were fed extensively to goldfish, as well as to such food fishes as Carp and Rainbow Trout. With the advent of synthetic fibers, silk production has dropped sharply and the almost limitless supply of inexpensive silkworm chrysalides is no longer available. Other live foods, such as *Daphnia* and *Tubifex* worms, are also becoming less available as their natural habitats are being eliminated through building, reclamation projects, contamination or insecticide poisoning.

Fortunately, research has produced prepared foods which are available to the commercial breeders as well as the hobbyist and which, to a large extent, reduce the necessity for feeding live foods. Even though live food is difficult to obtain at times, it is advisable to feed it occasionally in order to encourage optimum growth and health. Goldfish have lived for years in bowls and aquariums on a diet of commercial dried food, but their growth, color and finnage did not compare with that of fishes whose diet was supplemented with live food.

For certain types of goldfish such as the Lionhead, and for the newborn fry of all varieties, some live food in the diet has, so far, been indispensable. If the Lionhead diet does not include a large

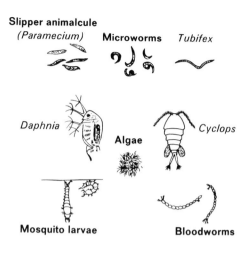

Slipper animalcule
(Paramecium)   Microworms   Tubifex

Daphnia   Algae   Cyclops

Mosquito larvae   Bloodworms

proportion of such foods as *Tubifex* worms and bloodworms, the fish will not develop their Lionhead characteristics. If newborn fry are not fed finely sieved *Daphnia* or newly hatched brine shrimp for the first weeks of their life, they will not grow properly. However, most goldfish beyond the fry stage seem to do quite well with prepared foods or home recipes.

Eggs on nests should not be put in ponds with heavy populations of *Daphnia*. Adult *Daphnia* may feed on the eggs, wiping out the entire spawning. In addition, the respiration of the *Daphnia* may deplete the oxygen.

A listing of all the existing live foods would be a long one indeed. However, as many are not readily obtainable, or are difficult to handle, we will confine ourselves to a discussion of some of the more popular ones.

Daphnia

Daphnia are small crustaceans belonging to the order *Cladocera*. They are found in fresh water all over the world. Many small related crustaceans are lumped under the heading of *Daphnia* by aquarists, and these may include not only the different species of *Daphnia*, but also the related *Cyclops* and other types. It is not surprising to hear discussions of red, pink, gray, green or white *Daphnia* without the speaker realizing that they may be of different species or even genera, or that small crustaceans may pick up their colors from their diet or environment. Because so many crustacea comprise this group, they are frequently lumped together under the designation "daphnid."

Daphnia have been a longtime favorite for raising goldfish as well as other types of aquarium fish. They were once particularly favored—at least before the growth of suburbia filled in the ponds and marshes—because they were so readily available and cost no more than the effort that it took to gather them; but it is becoming increasingly difficult to find *Daphnia* ponds. Still, diligent hunting may turn them up in the most unlikely places.

Fortunately, newborn *Daphnia* are small enough to be eaten by the smallest goldfish fry. *Daphnia* reproduce readily under the proper conditions, which includes a water temperature above 68°F. When conditions are right, each daphnid will lay 15 to 25 eggs in its brood chamber every two to three days. All daphnids hatching from these eggs are female. In less than one week, the newly hatched daphnids become adults and will start laying their own female eggs. A daphnid life cycle is about forty days. *Daphnia* will continue to reproduce in this way as long as the water temperature is proper and there is an adequate supply of phytoplankton for them to feed upon. Even while the *Daphnia* are reproducing freely under these optimum conditions, an occasional male will be born. The male will fertilize the eggs within the female. These eggs are known as *ephippia* or "winter eggs." If the food supply gets low or the water temperature drops, the female will lay these blackish winter eggs, after which she will die. The winter eggs remain on the pond bottom in the mud—and even survive drying—until, with the warm rains of spring, conditions become favorable for hatching.

The term for the production of all female *Daphnia* is "monogenesis," while the production of the winter eggs, which are fertilized by the male *Daphnia* is called "bisexual reproduction."

Commercial *Daphnia* raising is discussed elsewhere, but in this section I would like to explain how *Daphnia* may be raised at home in a small pond or aquarium.

Make a paste of six ounces of manure (well-rotted cow manure is best), two ounces of yeast and 18 pounds of clay. Put this into a large empty aquarium or tub. Let the paste dry out thoroughly in sunlight, and then half fill the vessel with water. Introduce a

In order to develop a champion Lionhead like this, the diet should include a large proportion of live foods.

few *Daphnia* and in about one week they should be producing rapidly.

When the reproduction of *Daphnia* seems to be slowing down, crush about one quarter of a fresh yeast cake in three ounces of water and shake or mix it until a fine suspension is formed. This amount will feed a 5- to 20-gallon culture for five or six days. Green water can also be added as food since the *Daphnia* feed on the phytoplankton or single-celled algae which make the water green. In fact, experienced aquarists clear green water by adding more *Daphnia* than the fish can eat. Adequate aeration must be provided, though, as *Daphnia* are heavy consumers of oxygen.

A word of caution: when gathering *Daphnia* from wild ponds, there is always the risk of introducing undesirable parasites and predators, even though we try to screen all of these out of our *Daphnia* catch. Place your collection in a shallow white enamel basin and check it carefully before introducing any into the aquarium.

Collecting *Daphnia*

Daphnia are collected with long-handled nylon nets, with the bag attached to the net rim by rings rather than sewn on. This reduces damage to the net, which is swished through the water in a figure-eight movement. The bottom of the net should be rounded rather than having it come to a point. This prevents the collected mass from compacting.

Remember, *Daphnia* require a great deal of oxygen, so don't collect more than you can safely transport or you may lose everything. Use polystyrene or plastic foam containers with a little ice to help prevent overheating and reduce mortality during transportation.

Tubifex Worms

Tubifex are a species of tube worm in the family *Tubificidae*. As with *Daphnia*, there are several species as well as several closely related genera, notably *Limnodrilus*. Although popularly known as *Tubifex*, collectively they should be referred to as tubificids. Tubificid worms are found in shallow, slow-moving waters. As you approach such waters, you will see them in clumps, their small, slender tails protruding from their tubes in the mud and waving to and fro. When startled, the whole colony of worms will retract immediately, leaving no trace of their presence. Tubificids thrive in water which we would call stagnant or, even worse, in waters containing large amounts of sewage. They are nature's water purifiers.

When collecting *Tubifex* worms, the mud and all must be taken, and the worms separated from it. Scoop a quantity of mud containing the worms and place it in a shallow pan, about 1½ feet square and 3 inches deep. The worms will rise to the surface after a period of hours. Because some worms will clump and leave the pan, it is best to provide for catching this overflow. However, because of the unpleasant habitat in which *Tubifex* live, the collecting of them is best left to professionals.

Tubificid worms do put very good growth on young fish, but for fry two or three weeks old, the *Tubifex* worms should be chopped up with a razor blade and rinsed before feeding.

To cleanse the worms, they are often put into a shallow container with two or three tablespoons of powdered dry milk for a couple of hours, after which they are put under running water. The powdered dry milk causes the tubificids to purge themselves of any noxious matter they may contain.

Tubifex will live for several days—although they will not reproduce—in a shallow pan under a gently running stream of water. Clean them daily by pouring the water off, then sliding the mat of worms carefully into another container. Finally, the accumulated slime and dead worms below the mat of living worms are thoroughly rinsed away. An alternative method of keeping small quantities of *Tubifex* alive for a period of weeks is in a shallow pan kept in a refrigerator. This should be large enough so that when the worms form the typical mat, there is space between the worm mass and the edges of the pan. Kept this way, only enough water is required to keep the *Tubifex* moist. A stream of cold water should be directed onto the clump daily to break it up. Then the same procedure as outlined above is followed to clean the pan.

If the water turns red, or the worms gray, best dispose of the lot.

Tubificid worms have a tendency to bury themselves in the aquarium gravel; therefore, no more should be fed at any one time than the fishes can consume.

Tubifex feeders are shallow plastic perforated saucers which float at the surface of the water. As a lump of worms is placed in them, individual worms slowly crawl through the perforations to the fish waiting below. If there are quite a number of fishes in the tank, more than one feeder may be necessary. An alternative method of feeding is to take a small clump of worms between your fingers, or with forceps, and swish them back and forth through the aquarium water, so that the worms separate and drop down individually.

Bloodworms (*Chironomus* Larvae)

Bloodworms are larvae of the *Chironomus* fly. They are about $\frac{1}{4}$- to $\frac{1}{2}$-inch long and are easily recognized by their bright red color. Their presence is usually detected by the cylindrical tube-shaped nest that they make. One way to collect them is by fastening an end of a small watchspring on the end of a stick. With the spring, cut under the tubes where the bloodworms are likely to be and they will probably coil themselves around the spring. They can then be lifted out of the water and put into the collecting bucket.

Another method of collecting bloodworms is to gather the

larvae with as little of the surrounding mud as possible, and place the mud and larvae in a sieve which is kept floating on the surface of the water. The bloodworms will work their way through the meshes of the sieve and then can be collected from the bottom of the container.

Bloodworms come from a less noxious environment than do *Tubifex*, so there is not too much danger attendant in feeding them to our fish. They can be kept alive at room temperature for a day by placing them between two sheets of damp newspaper, and if kept in a pan with shallow water at a temperature of 45° to 50°F, they will live for some time. The worms should be poured into a net and the water changed daily.

Mosquito Larvae

Mosquito larvae are a good dietery supplement for fish from three or four weeks told to the largest adult. At one time it was easy to gather a supply of mosquito larvae from any stagnant ditch or puddle, but today, in an effort to keep down the mosquito population, most stagnant water is sprayed by the authorities. It is easy enough to raise mosquito larvae just by leaving a basin outdoors with a few leaves or some other vegetation decomposing in it. The basin will soon be visited by the female mosquito, who lays the egg rafts from which the wrigglers will be hatching out. You will be performing a public as well as private service, because in addition to cutting down on the mosquito population by taking a certain amount of eggs out of circulation, you are supplying your fish with one of the most trouble-free live foods. However, in spite of these benefits, a few words of caution are in order: don't let your neighbors know what you are doing—they may not understand—and don't forget about your mosquito basins or you will soon have some unpleasant reminders.

Surplus larvae should be also be kept refrigerated to prevent metamorphosis.

Brine Shrimp

These small shrimp are found throughout the world wherever natural or artificial factors produce bodies of water with extremely high salt concentrations, such as the Great Salt Lake in Utah, or salt farms in California where large pools are evaporated in the sun in order to concentrate the salt. The eggs are collected and dried, in which form they can remain viable for years. At the present time, all shrimp egg processing is carried out in the United States or Canada; from these two countries the eggs are shipped all over the world.

While the adult brine shrimp makes good food for larger goldfish, the newly hatched shrimp or *nauplii* are even more important as a first food for goldfish which have just hatched. Even in Japan, where shrimp eggs are rather expensive, since they must all be imported, they are used as a basic food for young goldfish.

The food value of the *nauplii* is higher than that of the adult shrimp. The newly hatched shrimp provides a complete diet, requiring no supplementation, but goldfish will not thrive on a diet composed exclusively of adult brine shrimp.

In some large cities, brine shrimp are raised to adult size and sold commercially by portions in cups of salt water. Of course, the shrimp must be netted or otherwise separated from the brine and rinsed before feeding them to the fish. They will live six to eight hours in fresh water. Excess shrimp may be kept in salt water under aeration or in the refrigerator for several days.

The quality or percentage of hatchability of brine shrimp eggs seems to vary with the producing center and with the way that

Brine shrimp hatcher (pan method). The feeding rings are used to prevent the eggs from spreading over the surface; the baster tube is for sucking up the nauplii; the side with the eggs should be covered to darken it.

F. N. GHADIALLY

the eggs have been processed. To hatch the shrimp, the eggs are placed in a solution containing eight tablespoons of salt per gallon of water at a temperature of 70° to 80° F. Heavy aeration is desirable; hatching takes place in 24 to 48 hours. These *nauplii* are so small that we may have difficulty recognizing them at first, but they will be seen to have a pinker color than the eggs, and if we take a little of the solution out in a test tube and hold it against the light, we can see the tiny shrimps swimming about. Brine shrimp *nauplii* are phototropic; that is, they will be attracted towards light. This tendency is utilized to separate the brine shrimp from the unhatched eggs and empty shells. Wedge a strip of wood or plastic across the width of a narrow pan so as to divide it roughly in half. The strip should extend above the water and be raised about $\frac{1}{2}$-inch from the bottom. The eggs are placed on one side of this divider and the area is then covered so as to darken it. The brine shrimp as they hatch will swim under the divider toward the light, where they may be siphoned off. Another method of separating the brine shrimp is to shut off the aeration: the shrimp should gather in a pink ball or cloud within the hatching jar, from which they can be carefully siphoned off into very fine netting.

In comparision to *Daphnia*, brine shrimp are more troublesome to raise and, of course, more expensive. Because of this they are used primarily by city dwellers and others who do not have ready access to *Daphnia*, and fed to the young goldfish fry only until such time as they are ready to take other less expensive food.

One final compliment should be given to brine shrimp as a food for young fish, and that is that it is the least likely of the live foods to carry diseases or parasites.

Microworms

These are very small white worms which can be used to supplement the diet of goldfish when they are about two weeks old. Microworms can be raised in small covered containers such as glass jars or plastic boxes about four inches across. It is best to start with a culture obtained from a dealer or a fellow fancier. Raising microworms is very simple, although unfortunately some find the smell of the culture unpleasant. To prepare the culture, place a thin layer of uncooked oatmeal which has been thoroughly soaked in water in the bottom of the container. On top of this

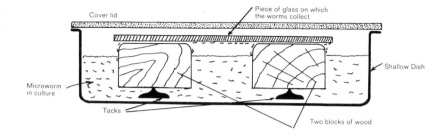

JIM KELLY

A homemade microworm incubator. The blocks of wood and piece of glass are not necessary; the worms can be scraped from the sides.

place a piece of yeast about as big as the joint on one's thumb. The premeasured packets of dried yeast are just about the correct amount for a microworm culture. The starter culture of microworms is added to this and the container kept loosely covered. In a day or two, a white film will form on the sides of the container. This film is made up of thousands of tiny microworms which can be scraped off with a knife blade and fed to the young fry. Any time from five days to two weeks later the microworm culture will reach a stage where the worms are not readily reproducing, and then it is time to start a new culture. Pour a little of the liquid from the old jar into it and the new culture will soon be flourishing.

Earthworms

When conditioning fish for breeding, one of the foods which are generally available to the fancier is the earthworm. From the tiny worms which can be fed whole to the larger fish to the large nightcrawlers which must be chopped up, earthworms are an excellent food. They can be obtained during most seasons of the year when the ground is not frozen, but the difficulty of getting earthworms during dry spells has prompted some fanciers to raise their own in order to have a more dependable supply. Earthworms are raised quite easily and dealers in fishing bait will sell a supply of these worms along with instructions for raising them. Fishing magazines carry advertisements offering earthworms for mail order sale, or you can just gather your own worms and keep them at cool temperatures (about 65°F) and in a dark place. A recommended food for their culture is a mixture of lard and cornmeal. Place a little of this in a depression in the sod and replace as necessary. The box should be covered to keep the soil moist.

Prepared Foods

As we have seen, some live food is essential for fry starting out in life and for the proper development of certain characteristics, such as the cap on Ranchūs and Orandas. But it is not practical for most of us to feed live food as frequently as we would like, so we must resort to various prepared foods as a substitute for, or as a supplement to, an occasional feeding of live food.

When goldfish are kept indoors, they require a much better quality food than do goldfish kept in outdoor quarters, where sunlight will help grow algae on which the fish can feed, and where each day brings a fresh supply of protein in the form of various insects in the water. One hears of goldfish being successfully kept in ponds on a diet of white bread only, but the fishkeeper who claims this does not realize nature has been steadily supplementing the inadequate diet.

Live foods such as those found in ponds outdoors usually contain all of the nutritive elements needed for the life and health of our goldfish, so we do not need to concern ourselves with the composition of those foods. However, when feeding prepared foods, it is well to have at least a sketchy idea of their composition in order to be able to determine what constitutes an adequate diet.

Trout Foods

It is unfortunate that research on goldfish nutrition is not as far advanced as research on other animal feeds. There has been some excellent work done on trout foods in order to find formulas which would promote fast growth and good health. The trout raiser is as much concerned as the cattle farmer in getting the best return for his time and money, and competition among the food producers, along with help from the government fisheries bureau, has led to the marketing of some excellent trout foods. Requirements for trout and other salmonoid fish are naturally not identical to those for goldfish, but it has been found that trout food can be used in a goldfish diet; these foods are made more suitable for goldfish if they are modified by adding some vegetable or other carbohydrate matter to them.

Goldfish are normally browsing animals and consume a great deal of vegetable matter; their intestine shows this, being longer than that of the more carnivorous fish. Normally, protein digestion takes place in the stomach, but as Carps have no true stomach, the gullet opens directly into the intestine. This is an indication of how well goldfish are equipped to digest carbohydrates and fibrous matter.

Food Components

As with most living things, food for goldfish must contain protein, fat, carbohydrates, minerals and vitamins, and in the proper proportions.

Proteins

Proteins are composed of amino acids. Approximately twenty-one of these have been isolated, but it is probable that not all of these are necessary to life. Those which are, are termed the "essential amino acids." The number and proportion of these acids in a given food determine the value of the food. Proteins are the building blocks of which the essential tissues of goldfish are formed, and we are mainly concerned that any prepared goldfish food does contain the necessary protein. A good food should contain at least twelve per cent protein. In the digestive system of the goldfish protein is broken down into amino acids.

Fats

Fats and carbohydrates are the sources of energy for the goldfish. They might be considered the fuel on which goldfish run. When fats and carbohydrates are somewhat lacking in the goldfish diet, but where there is a good supply of protein food, the protein can be used as a source of energy (calories) in addition to its function as tissue-building material. Again, not enough research has been done for us to say what amounts of fats and carbohydrates should ideally be contained in a formula for goldfish food, but based on present knowledge we would tentatively recommend a minimum of 4 per cent fats and 45 per cent carbohydrates.

Fats are broken down into fatty acids and glycerides in the intestines, in which form they are absorbed into the body, the excess being stored by the body as tissues. Fatty tissues are also made up of the carbohydrates and proteins which are ingested by the fish in excess of its daily requirements for growth and energy and which are converted to fat. In addition to serving as a store-house or reservoir of energy, the fatty tissues also store the fat-soluble vitamins A, D, E, and K.

An excess of fat or fat-producing foods is harmful to goldfish because it can cause malfunctions of the kidneys and lead to fatty degeneration of the liver. Foods containing large amounts of fats should be avoided, particularly when the water temperature is low, since the fish's metabolism and food needs slow down.

At no time should we feed goldfish food which is suspected of having deteriorated, since oxidized or rancid fats are harmful fish feed. Some work has been done in testing the best types of fat for use in foods for tropical fish, but there the problem is somewhat simpler. Tropical fish are kept at fairly constant temperatures, whereas the ideal goldfish food may vary with the seasons of the year.

Carbohydrates

Carbohydrates, which are the starches and sugars in the food, serve as a source of energy in themselves and they are also believed to aid in the utilization of fat by the goldfish, although the full role of carbohydrates in fish diets has never been satis-factorily defined. The digestive systems of fish which feed almost exclusively on animal matter are not designed for the most effective utilization of carbohydrates. Their intestines are relatively short, since protein foods are digested in a shorter period of time than are carbohydrates. On the other hand, fish which feed to a large degree on vegetable matter—such as the goldfish—must have a digestive system which can handle carbohydrates efficiently, since the nutri-tive parts of many plants consist largely of carbohydrates. In addition to their nutritive value, carbohydrates also help to produce the body shape which is sought after in some types of goldfish, such as Ryūkin, where a short, plump body shape is desirable.

In the intestines, carbohydrates are broken down into simple sugars, in which form they may be absorbed or stored in the liver and other organs. However, if too much glycogen (a simple sugar) is absorbed into the liver, it becomes enlarged and goldfish can die from this condition. Often, prized goldfish are fed too heavily in an effort to promote growth and encourage the development of a pleasing round shape, but then—apparently in prime condition—the fish suddenly shows signs of distress, spends its time on the bottom and eventually dies a lingering death. While the health of the fish in this condition is deteriorating, it may become dropsical in appearance, with protruding scales. This condition comes on suddenly and, unfortunately, by the time we notice something is wrong, the condition is irreversible.

Minerals

Minerals, such as calcium, magnesium, iron, copper and phosphorus, are necessary for the good health of our fish. Some of these are needed in minute amounts, but if they are missing, the organic balance of the fish is upset. In addition to the more

Many people consider the Oranda Shishigashira, or "Oranda" as it is popularly known, to be the most beautiful of all goldfish varieties.

common minerals mentioned, it is likely that traces of otner minerals serve a necessary, but as yet undefined, role in maintaining health. The best way to insure that our fish are receiving the mineral elements they need is to give them a varied diet.

Vitamins

Vitamins are indispensable to the goldfish, just as they are to the human diet. When fresh food and unprocessed vegetable matter are included in fish diets, the vitamin requirements will automatically be met, but when our fish must rely on prepared foods, it is an absolute requirement that these foods be vitamin enriched. One in particular, carotene or pro-vitamin A, is essential to the proper coloring of our fish. This is found in deep green algae, egg yolk and the shell of shrimp, particularly pink shrimp.

Balance the Diet

The Veiltail, like the other deep-bellied fishes, quickly reacts to a poorly balanced diet, becoming lean and hungry-looking when confined to a diet of earthworms (high protein), for example, and fat and lazy on a diet of oatmeal (high carbohydrate). Breeders favor the recirculation of water for this reason; the currents set up keep the fish on the move, which in turn helps to burn up the excess carbohydrates. The deep-bellied fishes must be kept under continuous observation and their diets adjusted so that they preserve a good rounded body, which does not make them ideal pond fishes. For this reason, Veiltails reared in ponds are never as good as those reared in large aquariums.

Carps and Cows

As a matter of fact, researchers studying Carp nutrition have concluded that their degree of digestion is astonishingly similar to that of a cow. The digestive enzymes of a Carp are only one eighth as efficient at digesting protein as are those of a Pike, which is carnivorous, while the Carp's carbohydrate digestion is 1,000 times more efficient than that of a Pike. On the other hand, researchers have learned that a fish's ability to digest certain foods is improved with familiarity; that is, if it is fed the same foods regularly it digests them better. Based on this, it would seem that any change in our fish's diet should be made gradually, and no more often than necessary.

Supplementing a fish's diet can be done at any time. This is particularly valuable when live food is the supplement. It seems that live food contains factors which are necessary to our fishes' well-being, and apparently even small quantities can supply enough of these vital factors to make a difference in the overall nutrition of the fish.

Dry Food

As a practical matter then, what types of dried or dehydrated foods should we use for our goldfish? In years past the fish foods offered in shops were often grossly inadequate, and knowledgeable breeders and fanciers used various mixtures of their own making. Today, the quality is much better, due in part no doubt to the keen competition among food manufacturers. The protein content as given on the label is a rough guide as to the quality of the food. A rule of thumb is that the greater the amount of protein in the formula, the better the food—minimum of 12 per cent and up to 18 per cent. Also note the variety of ingredients used. The more ingredients in the formula, the more likely it is to be a good one. Also, it is reassuring if a good part of the mixture comes from the sea, as these are more likely to be easily assimilated and to contain the various trace minerals.

There are many brands of fish foods available, and if one relies on these prepared foods to a large extent, it would be an excellent practice to purchase a number of different brands and vary the diet.

Frozen and Freeze-dried Foods

Our modern technology has spawned a host of developments, all of them helpful to the hobby of fishkeeping. The development of "frozen meals" for the home has been paralleled by the development of frozen fish foods. Today, in many places, shrimp, *Daphnia*, *Tubifex*, bloodworms and mosquito larvae, as well as other live foods, are available frozen on a year-round basis. To feed, simply break off the required amount and drop it into the water. The balance should be kept frozen for future use. Caution! Once thawed out, these foods should not be refrozen.

In addition to these "for fish only" foods, there are human-type foods which can be beneficially fed to our fish. These include frozen shrimp, clams, lobsters, mussels and other seafoods. A chunk can be thawed out and hung by a string in the water for our fish to pick at (remove the excess after an hour or so), or the softer, more pulpy types can be shredded or chopped into fine portions for direct feeding.

Freeze-drying involves dropping the temperature of the food to be prepared to a sub-zero level and vacuum-removing the crystallized water. This modern method of food preparation does not destroy the cellular structure, as is usually the case with ordinary freezing. Experiments with such foods as freeze-dried shrimp and *Tubifex* seem to indicate that this method preserves the essential nutritive values and the food can be stored in a container for an indefinite period of time with no special care. Regardless of the merit of these claims, the fact remains that the fish love the freeze-dried foods and they provide a valuable supplement.

Even though foods put out for the fanciers of goldfish and tropical fish are of good quality and getting better as time goes by due to continuing research, there are still many fishkeepers who prefer to make up their own preparations. These homemade formulas are relatively inexpensive and if a large collection of goldfish must be fed, the economics of feeding may encourage the use of homemade food for our goldfish. With many of us, I suspect that the motive in making up our own formulas from a little of this and that is not so much to cut down on our food bills —which are not significant unless we are breeding on a commercial basis—but to feel that we are taking a more personal interest in our fish by making up their food ourselves. Any good mother enjoys watching her children eat, and her pleasure comes in large part from knowing she has made the food for them herself.

For those who want to make up their own special food mixtures, some of the formulations which have been used over the years by goldfish fanciers are listed.

A Meal-Gelatin Diet for Aquarium Fishes

Details for this formulation were presented at the Aquarium

Symposium of the American Society of Ichthyologists and Herpetologists, Miami, Florida, June 21, 1966 by Edward J. Peterson, Acting Director, National Aquarium, Washington, D.C.; Rayburn C. Robinson, Aquarist, National Aquarium, Washington, D.C. and Harvey Willoughby, Assistant Chief, Division of Fish Hatcheries, Washington, D.C.

Ingredients	Per cent	Quantity
Water	48	1440 cc
Trout Diet in Meal Form	25	750 gm
Liver, Shrimp or Clams	12	360 gm
Animal Gelatin		
(Commercial Grade)	10	300 gm
Vitamin A & D Feeding Oil	5	150 cc

Directions

(1) Drain flavoring ingredients and blend these with feeding oil in a blender. Add 200 cc water or liquid drained from flavoring ingredients;

(2) Dissolve animal gelatin in 1240 cc hot water (200°F), beating with electric mixer until smooth, lump-free mixture is attained, while the mix cools to 150°F;

(3) Add flavoring ingredients (Step 1 above) and meal to the dissolved gelatin. Mix at low speed. Other ingredients such as food coloring, special nutrients or antibiotics can be added at this time;

(4) Pour into shallow trays and cool. Store in refrigerator until needed. The mixture is quite rubbery and can be shredded or chopped into appropriate sizes for feeding.

The authors claim that this formula is easy to cut, shred and store; decreases the need for live food; is accepted readily by the fish; aids in reducing tank turbidity and helps to insure near-maximum delivery of nutrients to the fish.

The principal ingredient used at the Aquarium was trout diet, which is available in dried form from a number of manufacturers of trout foods. However, any good dried aquarium food can be substituted.

Gordon's Formula

The late Dr Myron Gordon, who was Fish Geneticist with the New York Zoological Society for many years and an active aquarist himself, used the following formula for feeding his tropical fish. It is also suitable for feeding to smaller goldfish. The quantities given may be modified to suit special needs.

Remove the blood vessels, connective tissue and other fibrous material from one pound of beef liver, and cut it into $\frac{1}{2}$-inch cubes. A scissor is handy for this.

Taking small quantities of liver at a time, add equal amounts of cold water and blend them in a high-speed blender. The resulting liquid should be strained into a large bowl. Add two teaspoons of non-iodized salt.

To this add 20 tablespoons of a precooked baby cereal such as Pablum, and stir thoroughly.

Fill small glass containers, such as baby food jars, but do not cover them. Place them in a pan of water and bring the water to a boil. Allow the jars to remain in the water for half an hour after the heat has been turned off and when they have cooled, cover them and keep refrigerated or frozen.

Small portions (the size depending on the number and size of the fishes) may be fed as often as desired. The advantage of this formula is that the blood will not leach out into the water, and a lump placed on the bottom of the aquarium will be picked at by the fish all day long. The uneaten portion may be removed in the evening.

How Much Food?

Gauging the exact amount of food to feed is a matter of skill and practice. The amount the fish will eat varies with the period of time since he's had his last meal, the temperature of the water, the amount of dissolved oxygen in the water, the amount of pollutants in the water, the size of the fish, how much natural food is available, as well as a host of other factors.

The most workable approach is to feed your fish just a little and watch to see how fast it is consumed. If it disappears quickly with the fish showing no sign of slowing down their feeding rate, add a little more; continue doing this until they show signs of losing appetite. After a few feedings, you will have a fairly good idea of how much your fish can take in any given meal.

There is more danger in overfeeding than in underfeeding.

Overfeeding means that fish are given more than they can consume in a given time. Except in the case of certain live foods, which will remain alive until they are eaten, excess food will rot and pollute the water. Thus a necessity for feeding small amounts gradually.

On the other hand, fish can live a long, long time on a maintenance diet. They will remain the same size if the crowding and diet are carefully regulated. Growth resumes when more space and food are provided.

Some signs of pollution due to overfeeding are: smelly water, gray cloudy water, slimy mulm on the bottom, gravel turning black and cotton-like puffs in the aquarium. The latter are fungus spores growing on rotten food.

How Often to Feed the Fish?

Fish have a fairly rapid digestion, and if maximum growth is desired they should be fed every six hours or so. In fact, if a light is left on continually, they can be fed right through the night. Such intensive feeding, which forces growth, is neither necessary nor desirable. Fish in outdoor pools should be fed once a day or, if there are few fish in a considerable quantity of water, every other day or three times a week during the growing season. To avoid the risk of overfeeding, it is best to feed goldfish in aquariums once a day.

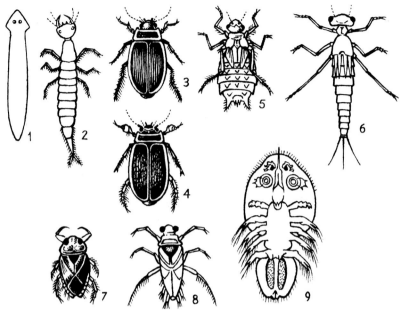

Fish enemies (not drawn to scale): (1) Planarian. (2), (3) and (4) Larva, adult male and adult female of the Great Diving Beetle (*Dytiscus marginalis*). (5) Larva of the Dragonfly (*Epitheca bimaculata*). (6) Larva of the Dragonfly (*Erythromma najas*). (7) Water Boatman (*Corixa geoffroyi*). (8) Backswimmer (*Notonecta glauca*). (9) Fish Louse (*Argulus* sp.).

IX   Diseases and Natural Enemies

When a goldfish has health problems, one of six reasons will generally be found to be the root of the trouble:

1. Careless changing of the water and rough handling.
2. Deterioration of the environment.
3. Improper food or overfeeding.
4. Transmission of disease from other sick goldfish.
5. Parasites.
6. Overcrowding.

If one takes normal precautions to prevent the above conditions, goldfish may be kept for years without ever showing signs of sickness.

Even though we may be conscientious about providing the proper conditions to keep our fish healthy, it is still important to keep a watchful eye on the behavior of the fish. When one has had a little experience in goldfishkeeping, a quick glance will often indicate when something is wrong, alerting us as if by a sixth sense to the onset of trouble so that steps can be taken to remedy the condition while there is still time.

Except at the coldest times of the year, healthy goldfish should be swimming about vigorously, always on the hunt for food. Even a fish which is excessively heavily finned and is normally less active because of the heavy burden can indicate by a drop in its level of activity that it is experiencing difficulties. A very hot summer day might cause fish to slow down in their normal activity and this too, though we might think it to be a more or less normal occurrence, can be a warning to us to give the fish some protection from the broiling sun.

The following symptoms can be indications of trouble develop-. ing:

1. No response to food at feeding time, or halfhearted attempts at feeding.
2. Rubbing against the sides and bottom of a pond or tank in such a way that they seem to be trying to scrape something off the body.
3. A loss of normal luster.
4. Swimming about in what appears to be an absent-minded or purposeless manner.
5. Constant lying on the bottom, or hanging at the surface.
6. Fraying or rotting of the fins; body lesions; spots or lumps on the fins or body.
7. Emaciation or, conversely, bloating.
8. Fins, particularly the dorsal and caudal, clamped tightly.
9. Pale, rather than bright red, gills.

In the majority of cases, if the fishkeeper notices the onset of disease, sick goldfish can be brought back to good health. It is always a sad experience to watch them die off one by one, in spite of vigorous efforts to cure them, because the disease has been allowed to progress too far.

There are different goldfish diseases, and before attempting cures it is first necessary to diagnose the cause of the trouble, so that the same conditions or diseases will not kill off the remaining fish.

Treating Aquariums

There are certain differences in diagnosing and treating diseases in ponds as opposed to aquariums.

In an aquarium, because there are relatively few hiding places the fish is constantly visible. A lack of appetite at mealtimes is readily noticed and often it is the first symptom alerting the keeper.

In a pool, a few sluggish fish often go unnoticed in an active crowd. This often gives the disease or other condition a chance to spread. Also, pool water is seldom as clear as aquarium water, and there are usually many more hiding places in a pool. Therefore, we must be even more alert and conscientious when inspecting our pools. Any fish which is not behaving normally should be dipped out and put into a clear glass container for closer examination.

While all of the diseases and problems described in this chapter can be found in either pool or aquarium, some are more common in one than in the other. For example, anchor worm, fish louse and, of course, natural enemies are more commonly found among pool fish, or among fish which have recently been transferred from the pool to the aquarium; on the other hand, *Ichthyophthirius* (ich), *Saprolegnia* (fungus), dropsy and flukes are of course likely to be found in a pool, but they are more noticeable in the aquarium.

The drugs used to treat these conditions are the same for both environments, but of course the dosage must be adjusted to the quantity of water.

We have tried to give a description of the symptoms by which they might be recognized; something of the history of the parasite where this knowledge might aid in its control; and also the treatment to be followed, whether it occurs in pool or aquarium.

Pet shops and aquarium departments stock a wide range of medications for treating the various aquarium conditions. The average aquarist, with one or two aquariums, is probably better off sticking to these commercial remedies, in terms of both price and convenience. The drug treatments given here are primarily for the benefit of the pool owner who requires large quantities of drugs to treat a body of water.

The Hospital Tank

If only one or two fish require treatment, it is best to isolate them. A small, unfurnished aquarium or even a large enamel basin, provided with an air release, will do. This should be in a quiet area with a stable temperature. Bright light is not desirable. When placing a fish in the hospital tank, it is best to use as much of its own water as possible to minimize the shock of the change.

The advantages of using a hospital tank are:

1. The chances of infecting the healthy fish are reduced.
2. A smaller quantity of drugs is required for the reduced amount of water.
3. Plants in the main tank will not be subject to any damage. (Some drugs affect plants adversely.)
4. Healthy fish tend to pick on sick ones. This is not cruel; it is nature's way of eliminating the unfit.
5. Once treatment is completed, the hospital tank water can be discarded and the container sterilized with hot water, thus keeping it sterile.

Ichthyophthirius multifiliis

This disease is commonly known as "ich" or white spot disease. White spot disease is one of the more common of the afflictions that can affect goldfish, but fortunately it is one of the more easily controlled diseases if it is not allowed to progress too far. The parasite which causes the "white spot" is widely distributed in nature. It can be in the water with healthy fish in what is apparently a dormant state and not cause any trouble. The onset of an active infection of white spot is sometimes brought about by the fish being shocked and weakened by too great a temperature change. It occurs most frequently in the spring and early fall, or after a heavy rain which lowers the temperature of the water too quickly.

As the name "white spot" would indicate, it is an easy disease to diagnose, for fine white specks cover the body of the afflicted

A young Lionhead showing the spots characteristic of ich. Readily visible on a dark fish, they are difficult to see on a light one.

fish. At this stage, the sick goldfish will slow down noticeably in its activity. As the disease progresses, the white spots will start to cover the head and gill surfaces of the fish, and at this stage the fish's difficulty in breathing will cause death.

For treatment of white spot disease, the following procedure may be followed: place the sick goldfish in a container; gradually raise the temperature to slightly over 76°F and increase the aeration; dissolve one level teaspoon of salt for each quart of water in the container.

If the disease has advanced too far to respond to the salt bath treatment, quinine sulphate may be used. Dissolve ½ teaspoon of quinine sulphate in each gallon of water in a container without plants. The fish can be left there for three weeks.

Another treatment is to soak the sick fish in a solution of glacial acetic acid at a strength of 1:5000 to 1:10,000 (one ounce to 40 gallons is approximately 1:5000) for about twenty minutes and then place the fish in clean water.

Still another method is to use a malachite green solution, a medicine commonly sold in pet shops for this purpose. Malachite green is a very convenient method when bought in the pre-measured solutions. However, when treating a large pond, it might be more economical to make a stock solution. Dissolve one gram (there are roughly 30 grams to an ounce) of malachite green in four ounces of water. Use one drop of this solution for every gallon of water. At this strength, malachite green is not harmful to the fish—they do not have to be removed from the water, nor does the water have to be changed after the treatment is over; but do not exceed the required dosage. The malachite green treatment can be repeated for two or three days, by which time the white spot disease should be cured.

In a pond where white spot disease frequently recurs, it would be advisable to disinfect the pond with milk of lime (chlorinated lime), first, of course, removing the fish. The pond then should be drained down and, before putting the fish back into the refilled pond, you must make certain that no trace of the disinfecting agent is left. The chlorine may be neutralized by adding a quantity of sodium thiosulphate equal to the amount of lime used after the lime has soaked in for a day or two.

The Anchor Worm (*Lernaea carasii*)—and attached to the goldfish.

Lernaea carasii, Anchor Worm

This parasite is a *Copepod*, an order of very small aquatic crustaceans. They get their name from the shape of the head, which is likened to the anchor of a ship. Anchor worms burrow their heads into the bodies of goldfish, and the rear of the pectoral fin or right behind the dorsal fin is a common place to find them. If the infestation of these parasites is heavy, several dozen may be found on various parts of the fish. When the anchor worm first takes hold, it appears to be a bony splinter protruding at an angle, and while easily visible to the naked eye it may pass undetected if the fish is not specifically examined for its presence. However, as the presence of the anchor worm irritates the fish, a bloody red spot will show where the anchor worm has fastened into the body.

Anchor worms grip the fish tenaciously, and while they can be removed with a tweezer, little pieces of flesh are often pulled out with them. Care should be taken when removing the anchor worm, particularly if it is fastened near the eye of the fish.

If one's collection is not too large, control of anchor worm can be achieved by picking them off the fish and then placing the fish in uncontaminated water. This method may have to be repeated more than once.

A chemical method for controlling anchor worms is the use of Dipterex (Dylox Neguvon). This chemical insecticide is soluble in water and does not seem to affect the fish adversely, nor does it destroy the growth of phytoplankton in the pond.

This product is marketed in different potencies; that is, 40 per cent, 50 per cent, 80 per cent and 98 per cent active, and is available in both liquid and powder form.

Dosages given here are for the 98 per cent active form. When using a lesser strength, increase the dosage proportionately; for example, double the amount when using the 50 per cent active, increase the dose by 20 per cent when using the 80 per cent, etc.

Anchor worms ordinarily reproduce from early spring to fall, but several treatments with Dipterex in the early spring seem to be effective in eliminating the anchor worm. The required amount of Dipterex should be dissolved in a quantity of water and then distributed evenly over the surface of the pond at a strength of one part Dipterex to three to five million parts water. One gram of the drug to each 250 gallons of water equals 1 ppm. For treatment, use one gram of 98 per cent active to 1,375 gallons water. This treatment may have to be repeated three times at seven-day intervals, making up a fresh solution each time, in order to completely eliminate the anchor worms. As Dylox is not stable in water, it will break down in a few days, thus eliminating the necessity for any water change.

Large commercial breeding operations seem to have more trouble with anchor worms than the individual fancier does. Fortunately, if one is extremely careful when introducing new fish into the pond, it is unlikely that he will ever have to contend with anchor worms.

Argulus sp., Fish Louse

The fish louse is the other member of the *Copepod* family which commonly afflicts the goldfish. Fish lice fasten themselves flat against the body of the fish, and since the lice are fairly translucent they may not be easily noticed. A goldfish heavily infested with fish lice can be weakened to such an extent by the loss of blood that it will die.

While this parasite is less than five mm long, it can be identified fairly easily. The time to check for fish lice is when one sees the goldfish rubbing themselves vigorously on the sides and bottom of the pond, as if trying to dislodge something from their bodies. In an effort to rid themselves of the fish lice, the goldfish often injure themselves and these injuries may prove more dangerous than the actual damage done by the fish lice.

Dipterex is also effective in combating fish lice, and may be used in the same strength as for anchor worms, also three times at seven-day intervals. This is necessary because the eggs survive the treatment but the emerging parasites are eliminated by the follow-ups.

If the treatment is administered in an aquarium, normally all the lice drop off in two hours. When this happens remove all the fish and plants, disinfect the tank and all of the equipment and return the fish. The plants should be kept quarantined for 14 days, after which it is safe to use them with fish.

For the hobbyist, however, probably the simplest way to eliminate fish lice is to remove them from the body and place the fish in water which is uncontaminated. A half-and-half solution of kerosene and turpentine helps in the removal of fish lice. When this is patted on the skin gently with a piece of absorbent cotton or a cotton-tipped swab, the parasites can be removed easily.

Saprolegnia spp ., Water Musk Disease, Fungus

In Japan, this is sometimes called Watakemuri, which would be translated as "cotton-wearing disease." The body surface of the goldfish afflicted by this disease appears to be covered with tufts of cotton. Frequently mistaken for ich, this is a much more common problem. *Saprolegnia* is ubiquitous in the aquarium, but seldom seems to attack a fish unless its surface defenses are first weakened by injury or stress. It is a fungus, in the same class as bread mold. Low water temperatures themselves may make the fish prone to fungus attacks, since *Saprolegnia* occurs very often in early spring, in the colder part of the autumn and in winter.

If the fungus is allowed to spread, the skin and muscles of the goldfish will become inflamed and the fish will eventually die.

This same organism that attacks adult fish will infect goldfish eggs. It seems that it is primarily the dead eggs which are covered with the fungus, and it is not certain whether fungus causes any important losses of fertile eggs. The reason that the viable eggs are not affected too much is that frequently they have a relatively short hatching time. In certain species of fish, such as trout, where the eggs may take a long period of time to hatch, fungus is a serious problem and a fungicide is employed routinely.

Two medicines commonly used for the treatment of fungus are malachite green and copper sulphate.

Malachite green can be harmful if too much is used, and there are other factors to be considered, such as the size of the fish and how much they have already been weakened by disease. One treatment using malachite green is to bathe the sick fish in a solution of one part malachite green to four to five hundred thousand parts water for about two hours or less, and then change them into clean water.

Another method of applying malachite green is to put it into the goldfish pond at a ratio of one part of malachite green to three million parts water. This will not necessitate any change of water or later removal of the fish.

If one wishes to sterilize goldfish eggs to prevent fungus infection, they can be dipped into a solution of malachite green, one to two million to one to six million; but remove them immediately. Another way of treating the eggs is to use a weaker solution of one to six million and to soak the eggs for several hours.

Copper sulphate can be used to treat infected fish by making a solution of one part sulphate to two million parts water and keeping the infected fish in this for one to two minutes.

Potassium permanganate, one grain to ten gallons of water, has also been recommended. The water need not be changed; the purple discoloration disappears with time.

All of these drugs can weaken plants, although they usually recover.

Dropsy, Matsukasa

This disease is also called "setting-up-scales disease" and "pine-cone disease," because of the appearance of the fish. At the outset of this disease, the fish may fatten up slightly, but this does not usually alarm the fishkeeper. In the next stage of the disease, the scales start to protrude from the body because of the pressure of the accumulated body fluids.

The bacteria causing this disease are thought to be either *Vibriopiscium* or *Lepidorthae*. Unfortunately, a really effective treatment for dropsy has not yet been found, and although fish may live for several months, they seldom recover. There are differences of opinion as to whether dropsy is truly an infectious disease, since only occasional individuals are attacked and it does not seem to spread to other fishes as we would expect if the disease were highly contagious.

A goldfish affected by a severe case of dropsy. The rough, protruding scales characterize this disease.
AKIRA SUGI

Sometimes someone will record the cure of dropsy by one means or another, or note that the condition cleared up spontaneously. The reason for this may be that there is more than one condition which can cause the body to swell and the scales to distend; but in the great majority of cases when a fish appears dropsical it is doomed.

As a treatment for dropsy, antibacterials such as sulfadiazine or antibiotics like chloromycetin or terramycin are added to the water or mixed in the food. Another method is to put the fish into clean running water. However, these treatments are seldom successful.

Kihō byō, Foam Disease

Fish with foam disease present a very sad picture, but this is fortunately one affliction that is easily cured and easily prevented.

At times, heavy plant or algae growth, under the influence of strong sunlight, produces an overabundance of oxygen, saturating the water with this gas. As a result, foam may be seen adhering to the body and fins of the fish, causing them to become distressed, with a tendency to float to the surface of the water and lie on their sides because the surplus oxygen and nitrogen clogs their blood vessels. Often the short-finned fishes in the tank or pool will be completely unaffected, while the long-finned fishes are extremely distressed, probably because the longer-finned fishes have more circulation problems to begin with. If this condition is allowed to continue, the fish will die; but a simple treatment is to put the fish into clear water with no algae, or to at least change part of the water. Another method which will clear up the condition is to give the water heavy aeration with an air pump in order to restore the oxygen level of the water to normal.

Since foam disease almost always occurs in water that is dark green and in the presence of strong sunlight, it requires no great ingenuity to prevent its occurrence. When water is too dark green, that usually means that it is overpopulated with fish and that it is receiving too much sunlight. The remedy, then, is to cut down on the fish population or to shade the water, preferably both. Since we do not always want to cut down on the number of fish, or do not have additional facilities in which to house them, aeration from an air pump is a third alternative.

Flukes

There are two varieties of trematode worms which are parasitic to goldfish: gill flukes, or *Dactylogyrus*, and skin flukes, or *Gyrodactylus*. Both of these flukes are barely visible to the naked eye, and unless the infestation is heavy we can usually only suspect the presence of flukes by the behavior of the fish, which appear uneasy. If the flukes are on the fins, the fins will twitch; if inside the mouth, the fish will open and close its mouth quickly as if in an attempt to try to dislodge or blow something out of its mouth that is annoying it. The most usual symptoms are sudden movements of the fish as if startled, and then an attempt to rub or scrape itself on something in an effort to rub off the flukes. When the infestation is severe, large numbers of flukes may appear as a fuzzy patch on the body of the fish, or the gills may become so inflamed that they swell up and look white and puffy. If any fishes in a container or a pond are infected with flukes, it is safe to assume that all of the fish have flukes and require treatment.

The parasites are large enough to be seen with a low-power microscope, or even a strong magnifying glass. Under magnification, gill flukes may be seen at the edge of the gill cover as weaving threads.

Formalin ($37\frac{1}{2}$ per cent formaldehyde in solution) is one of the drugs recommended for treating flukes. Prepare a hospital tank by adding 20 drops of formalin to each gallon of water. Stir well before adding the infected fish. Meanwhile, a second solution should have been made up, consisting of a few ounces of water to which have been added 20 drops of formalin for each gallon of water in the hospital tank. Add this solution slowly to the tank over a period of ten minutes, stirring the water gently for an even dispersion. The fish should be left in this tank for another ten minutes, and then removed to clear water.

Another recommended method of using formalin is a twelve-hour bath in a one to 20,000 solution.

A quick dip in a glacial acetic acid solution of one to 400 is also effective for treating flukes. Fish should be left in this for only two minutes, for it is a strong remedy.

Gill flukes (*Dactylogyrus*) are particularly dangerous to young fry, especially under crowded conditions. An entire batch of fry can be killed off in two or three days by an infestation of gill flukes. Unfortunately, control of the flukes on young fry is extremely difficult, since the fry cannot stand the usual medication. The best way to prevent the loss of fry to flukes is to make sure that they are raised in fluke-free water. As a precaution, remove the eggs from the spawning pond, thoroughly rinse them and place them in clean water to hatch. In England, where gill flukes seem to have been a real problem, the recommended procedure is to disinfect the parent fish by treating them before permitting them to spawn in clean water. A drop of one part glacial acetic acid to 250 parts water is used. The sick fish is held in the net and dipped for 20 seconds only; treatment is repeated in a week.

Strong Salt Bath

A strong salt bath is one of the most effective methods of disinfecting goldfish, particularly when open sores caused by injury or parasitic infection leave the fish susceptible to secondary invaders. For example, a strong salt bath should be given after treatment for anchor worm or fish louse.

Use one pound of coarse salt to three gallons of water. Holding the fish in a net, dip it for 10 to 15 seconds, then promptly transfer it to fresh water. The fish may seem "knocked out" for a few minutes, but will soon recover. A slight shedding of mucus may take place; this does no harm.

Split Gut

Sometimes babies 10 to 20 days of age, a stage at which they are still transparent, will eat single-cell algae. On very clear, sunny days, the light will stimulate the algae *inside the babies* to produce oxygen, causing them to bloat and pop to the surface. In extreme cases the bubbles may be large enough to "split their guts." This, of course, will not occur after the babies have developed coloration, which protects them. "Split gut" has also been known to occur after the fish eat an excessive amount of certain dried foods.

Velvet (*Oodinium* sp.)

This is a protozoan parasite, somewhat similar to ich. Like ich, it has a free-swimming stage during which it actively seeks a host.

Not usually considered a disease of goldfish, it is frequently transmitted from an infected tropical fish tank.

The parasite, which is much smaller than the ich parasite, is almost invisible on golden goldfish; but it shows up readily on dark fish as a powdery, light tan covering. Goldfish which are heavily infested have a hazy appearance, and swim horizontally in a listless manner near the surface. In the latter stages they become emaciated before dying.

In the pool the copper sulphate treatment should be used for treatment. In an aquarium, use either copper sulphate (see *Saprolegnia*) or put ten copper pennies (American) to each gallon of water in the tank. Usually this effects a cure in 24 hours. Under certain water conditions the pennies may cause an excess of copper in the water, and this is indicated by the fish hanging with their mouths at the surface and distending their gills as they breathe. Should this occur, remove the copper pennies, siphon out and replace one third of the water, and add one teaspoon of salt for each five gallons of aquarium water. The fish will recover from the copper within a short time, with no further treatment.

Hanging at the Surface

Fish wallowing around, with their mouths "glued" to the surface, are a sure sign that all is not well. The usual causes are over-crowding and pollution. The latter can be caused by decomposing organic matter, which is usually, though not always, accompanied by a cloudy or milky tank; or it can be due to dissolved metals such as copper, due to overdosing or metal picked up by using water drawn from copper or brass pipes, usually new ones. Always run the water for at least fifteen minutes before using any. A third possible cause for "hanging" is gill flukes (see page 134).

Internal Diseases

There is seldom much that can be done for fish stricken with internal diseases. One exception is fish weakened by what is called indigestion or constipation. Indigestion occurs when goldfish are fed too heavily with food that cannot be readily digested. There is some doubt whether it is ever possible to overfeed goldfish if they are given proper food and kept under optimum conditions; however, since we seldom achieve optimum conditions for our fish, we know that overfeeding and bad food will cause disorders of the digestive tract which can be fatal.

When the intestines become inflamed from poor feeding they are no longer able to perform their proper function of digesting food and eliminating waste. In a healthy fish the feces are firm and solid, and often trail behind the fish in a long string, but when the digestive system is upset the feces become thin and watery looking. Some foods are more readily assimilated than others, and when fish are overfed the feces will clearly show food which has not been digested. While this is not as accurate a danger signal as thin and watery feces are, it does tell us that we are giving the fish so much food that it is being forced through the digestive tract faster than the system is able to utilize it.

The best protection against indigestion is to see that goldfish are always fed carefully. If the fish should fall prey to indigestion, best abstain from feeding them for a day or two. If practical, place them in water which is lightly salted at the rate of one teaspoon to one gallon of water. Epsom salts, one teaspoon to ten gallons of water, have also been recommended as an indigestion remedy, but since it can be a strong cathartic it should be used only when less drastic methods have proven ineffective. Live *Daphnia* or chopped earthworms are both naturally laxative, and they can be included in the goldfish diet, not only for their conditioning value but also as a precaution against constipation.

Injuries

Most goldfish injuries are due to our own rough or careless handling, although it is true that they may be injured accidentally, as for example when a fish has its scales scraped off during a vigorous spawning drive or when other fish, birds or aquatic insects snip off fins or take a chunk out of the fish's body.

If the injuries are not so severe or deep as to cause immediate death, they will usually heal by themselves, although there is always a danger that the injured part may become infected. To prevent diseases from gaining a foothold, swab the injured area with mercurochrome or cauterize it with a strong solution of potassium permanganate. Care should be taken not to get these

F. N. GHADIALLY

Injuries that are not promptly cared for can result in the fish's becoming infected. This is a bacterial fin rot—the fins are eroded, blobs and shreds of mucus are coming away from the body and fins and there is an ulcer on the gill cover.

medications in the fish's eyes or in its gills. It is also a good idea to remove the injured fish to a separate container, to allow it time to recuperate away from its healthy fellows. A teaspoon of salt to five gallons of water as an antiseptic in the recovery tank is a wise precaution.

Natural Enemies of Goldfish

We tend to think of insect life as being beneficial to goldfish kept outdoors, since we know that goldfish consume large quantities of mosquito larvae and aquatic insects as well as the myriad of flying bugs that fall into the water. But those who raise goldfish commercially and those hobbyists who have large outdoor pools know that there are some insects which turn the tables and dine on goldfish. Some water beetles in the adult and larval stage will attack goldfish as big as or bigger than themselves; the larvae of dragonflies and damselflies are notorious for this.

The insects are not readily detected, and often the first indication of their presence is numbers of fish mysteriously missing; or we may see fish with their tails bitten or otherwise injured. The only way to rid the pond of the unwelcome visitors is to drain it down and disinfect it. This should be done routinely every year, even though it may afterwards become reinfected with the larvae of flying insects. If practical, plants should also be disinfected, or else thoroughly inspected for the presence of the insect villains; but it is not always easy to note the presence of eggs lodged in the plants.

A way to prevent losses from insects, particularly among young fish, is to raise them in tubs or other containers. These can be kept covered, even though that is not the best method, since the covering will keep out all insect life, the bulk of which is welcome food for the young fish. A better method is to change the water in the tub or to put the fish into another tub of fresh water every two weeks. The insect larvae will not have time to grow to a dangerous size, and in addition the water change is beneficial to the health and growth of the young fish.

Cats

Cats can be present about goldfish pools for years without ever making any attempt to pull a fish out of the water (it is probably true that most cats never become fishers), but once they learn the knack they can clean out a small pond overnight. Often they will snatch out many more fish than they can possibly eat, and line the fish up in a neat row on the ground in some kind of a game which is amusing to cats but not to us—not when we find our fish lying about on the grass in the morning. It is difficult to feel kindly towards the fastidious cat who daintily bites the head off a fine Oranda. The only sure protection against cats, of course, is to keep the pool screened. When building a pond it is well to consider whether its design will permit us to arrange a cover easily. Chicken mesh is a good size, since this will permit the insects upon which the fish feed to fall into the water.

Frogs

Some species of frogs are great fish eaters, and can eat fish that are almost as big as themselves.

In some of the hatcheries in the USA, the frog population is kept down by shooting them. When the dead frogs are examined, they are often found to contain three or four goldfish.

A frog sitting on a lily pad in our pond can add to its picturesque beauty, but we must remember that the frog is not necessarily waiting for a passing fly and may have his mind on one of our best fish.

Insecticides

Today, people are aware of the dangers of indiscriminate use of insecticides, so just a word of caution will suffice. When spraying insecticides inside the house, cover the fish tank and shut off the air pump until the insecticide has settled out of the air. When spraying in the garden, make sure the wind is not carrying the spray over the fishpond.

Euthanasia

Sometimes, in spite of our best efforts, it becomes obvious that the case is hopeless and that it is best to destroy the fish. Many well meaning people "flush" the hapless specimen—thus, without meaning to, subjecting the fish to a cruel death of strangulation in some polluted sewer. The best method is dropping the fish into boiling water, as death as instantaneous.

Equivalents

Most people find it more convenient to buy packaged disease remedies and just follow directions. However, for those who prefer to "do it themselves," we have prepared a short table of equivalents which will, with a little study, enable the hobbyist with little or no scientific background to compute and use the treatments given in this book.

	Grains per British gallon	Grains per US gallon	Ounces per British gallon	Milligrams per liter	Grams per liter	Parts per 100,000	Parts per million
1 gr/British gal	1.0	0.83	—	14.0	0.014	1.43	14.3
1 gr/US gal	1.2	1.0	—	17.0	0.017	1.71	17.1
1 oz/British gal	480	387	1.0	6,660	6.66	666	6,660
1 milligram/liter	0.01	0.008	—	1.0	0.001	0.1	1.0
1 gm/liter	70.0	58.0	0.17	1,000	0.01	100	1,000
1 p/100,000	0.7	0.58	—	0.1	0.01	1.0	10.0
1 p/mil (ppm)	0.07	0.056	—	1.0	0.001	0.1	1.0

Table from Pet Fish Aquarist Diary

One English gallon = 5 quarts
One US gallon   = 4 quarts
One ounce (avdp.) = 28.3495 grams = 29.5737 cc
One US gallon   = 3.785 liters
One cc   = 20 drops
One teaspoon   = 5 cc
One tablespoon   = 3 teaspoons
One ounce   = 2 tablespoons = 6 teaspoons

Water weighs 8.3 lbs. per gallon. To compute the gallon capacity of a tank, multiply the length by the width by the height (in inches) and divide by 231.

A standard household bucket holds ten quarts.

The solid black color appears only on telescope-eyed fish, which would indicate that the gene for black color is linked to that for telescope eye.

X   Goldfish Genetics

Full-fledged studies on the genetics of goldfish were started in Japan by Dr Chiyomatsu Ishikawa and Dr Kametarō Toyama in 1898.

Later, goldfish research was carried on in other countries as well, and some of the early workers were Hans in 1914, Goodrich in 1924, and Hanson in 1921, all in the United States. In 1925 Berndt in Germany and, in the same year, Chen in China published the results of their studies. In Japan the significant findings were those published by Matsui, Ishihara and Kuwabara.

No discussion of the various types of Japanese goldfish would be complete without mentioning the famous breeder, Mr Kichigorō Akiyama, who introduced many new varieties with which Drs Ishikawa and Toyama were able to conduct their research.

In 1897 the Fisheries Institute, which today is the Tokyo University Bureau of Fisheries, took part in goldfish research, and the work of the Fisheries Institute was later carried on by Drs Higure and Matsui.

Scientists selected goldfish for genetic research because of the infinite number of mutants which arise, and because of the fact that they are readily domesticated. Further, large numbers of individuals can be obtained from a single spawning, thus giving geneticists large numbers of fish from which to average the count and on which to base their statistics. Against this must be weighed drawbacks. It takes one to two years for a goldfish to become sexually mature, and to raise any significant number of fish, large ponds are required. Some of the characteristics of goldfish take several years for complete development. Further, most of the characteristics which the geneticist would study are determined by multiple gene factors and, last but not least, it is not always certain that one has a genetically pure line of goldfish to start with, since there has been so much crossing of various types of fish.

If goldfish are not the ideal material for genetic research, at least they are rich in the special characteristics for producing new varieties, and I would like to outline some of the things that the geneticists have been able to tell us up to now about goldfish inheritance.

Inheritance of Telescope Eyes

In crossing fish from a strain which is pure for telescope eyes with fish from a strain which is pure for normal eyes, the fish born as a result of such a cross will all have normal eyes. This tells us that normal eyes are dominant over telescope eyes. The fish coming from the first cross, all having normal eyes, are now called the F_1 generation. When the F_1 fish are bred with each other, one quarter of the young fish will have telescope eyes and the remainder normal eyes. This is the classic ratio found by Mendel when dealing with simple dominant and recessive characteristics.

It has been found that by crossing a Crucian Carp with a domesticated telescope-eyed fish, the above three-to-one ratio does not work out. In these fishes, the ratio of normal eyes to telescope eyes in the F_2 generation is 15 to 1, and this is attributable to a factor present in the Crucian Carp which inhibits the formation of telescope eyes.

In the inheritance of telescope eyes, DD (dominant) is the genetic symbol for normal eyes; dd (recessive) the symbol for telescope eyes.

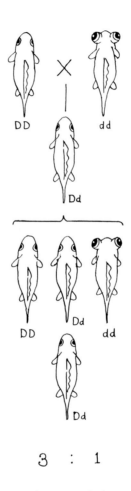

3 : 1

The genetic inheritance of telescope eye.

When we cross DD and dd, all the offspring of the first crossing (F_1) appear normal-eyed, but while the phenotype, which is the external appearance, is for normal eyes, the genotype, or genetic basis, has the gene for telescope eyes. The second crossing (F_2) produces the classic three-to-one Mendelian proportion, which results when a simple dominant is crossed with a simple recessive; three have normal eyes while one has telescope eyes. Of the three with normal eyes, one is pure DD while the other two carry the gene (d) for telescope eyes. Like all Mendelian proportions, this ratio may not be observed when small numbers are bred, but will be found true when averaged over larger numbers. This is expressed in chart form as follows:

$$dd \qquad \times \qquad DD$$

F_1 Dd (normal eyes in phenotype)

F_2 DD   2Dd   dd

normal eyes: telescope eyes $= 3:1$ (in phenotype)

The Funa (Crucian Carp), the ancestral type of the goldfish, has normal eyes, DD; in addition, however, it carries the genes AA which suppress the appearance of telescope eyes. Crossing the Funa with a telescope-eyed fish results in the first generation (F_1) all being normal-eyed, because they all have the repressor gene A. However, they all also carry the genes d and a as recessives.

When the F_1 are crossed brother to sister, their offspring (F_2) have a 15:1 ratio, normal to telescope eyes; only the fish having aadd will be telescope-eyed.

The F_2 cross may be blocked out as follows:

♀ \ ♂	AD	Ad	aD	ad
AD	AADD	AADd	AaDD	AaDd
Ad	AADd	AAdd	AaDd	Aadd
aD	AaDD	AaDd	aaDD	aaDd
ad	AaDd	Aadd	aaDd	aadd

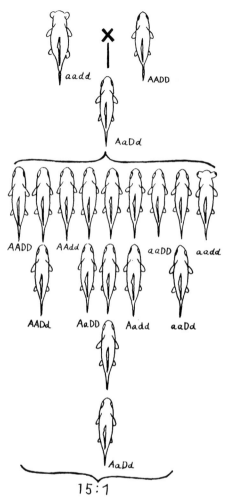

The function of the repressor gene in eye form inheritance.

Color

The basic colors of goldfish are black, red and yellow. Any other colors seen are these three colors in combination. The outer surface of a goldfish is made up of a retaining skin, the epidermis, scale and dermis; color pigment is found in any one of these layers. Thus, yellow pigment in the epidermis overlaying red pigment in the scale could give the fish an orange coloring.

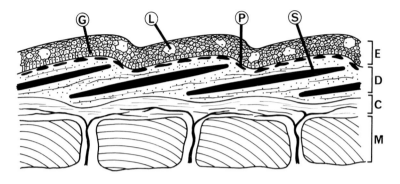

Diagramatic cross-section of the skin of a fish: (E) epidermis or outer layer, resting on (D) dermis. The subcutaneous connective tissue is shown as (C) and the muscles as (M). Basal or germinal cells (G) from which the epidermis regenerates and the slime or mucoid cells (L) are clearly defined. The pigment cells (P) lie at the dermo-epidermal junction. The scales (S) are embedded in the dermis.

Black pigment, to appear black, must lie in the epidermis, as transparent tissue overlaying black will appear as blue to the human eye. The deeper the black pigment is in the body, the paler the blue will appear.

With regard to the pigments themselves—the black and yellow pigments are allergic to the red pigments, which explains why Black Moors so often turn red. A few red pigments in a Black Moor will ultimately spread until they exclude the black pigments altogether, in which case a Black Moor will end up as a red fish. The best red metallic goldfish are those which pass from the wild gray coloring through a quick stage of black coloring before changing to red. The period during which the black dominates is merely a passing phase and may be as short as ten weeks.

Heredity of Body Color

Inheritance of color is a complicated subject which does not lend itself to genetic research easily. Usually, all that is done is to pick fish of the best color, breed them together and hope for the best. Generally speaking, white-colored goldfish are regarded as inferior and discarded early. Whether this has any real basis in fact is hard to say, but it has long been the custom to look down

The Shubunkin has both transparent and opaque scales.

upon white-colored fish, except in special varieties, such as Red-cap, Nankin Ranchū, etc., where the white color is a distinguishing feature of the particular variety.

Heredity of Scale Transparency

Goldfish have been classified as scaleless, partially scaled and scaled. Actually, all goldfish are covered with scales, but in the so-called scaleless fish the scales are transparent and not readily discernable. In the partially scaled fish some scales are transparent while others have the normal metallic luster, which comes from a silvery substance underlying each scale called guanine.

The opaque scales with metallic luster are seen on the Crucian Carp and on such varieties as Wakin and Ryūkin. Transparent scales are found on Sanshoku Demekins, Calicos, Shubunkins, etc. Neither the transparent scale nor the common scale is dominant genetically, and each will breed true to its group when properly mated.

When a transparent-scaled fish is crossed with a normal-scaled fish the young will show both types of scales. Actually, the fish we see with transparent scales usually have common scales mixed in among the transparent scales, indicating that it is a hybrid of the two scale types.

Fish with all transparent scales are not often seen commercially, probably because they do not show much intensity or variation in color and also because they are not hardy. Commercial breeders often cull out the all-transparent-scale fish from their broods.

The Goldfish Society of Great Britain has developed a terminology for the three types of fish: common (maximum shine)= metallic; transparent (no shine)=matt; mosaic transparent (dull mother-of-pearl shine)=nacreous. Using their terminology, we show in the diagram on page 151 the expected results from the crossing of scale types.

Netlike Transparent Scales

There is another type of scale, called the "netlike" or "reticular transparent" scale. While the scales we have talked about are either opaque because of a guanine backing or transparent because of a lack of guanine, scales found in the netlike transparent fish are *partially* backed with guanine. This gives these fish their distinctive netlike or reticulated pattern. Some individuals can be found among the netlike transparent fish which lack guanine completely, while others show so much guanine that they are hard to distinguish from normal fish. The amount of guanine present in these fish is probably due to the genetic makeup of the particular fish, although the American researchers Tippit and Bennet have shown that environment can also affect the amount of guanine.

These netlike transparent fish have been found among common goldfish, appearing apparently as spontaneous mutations. When these netlike transparent fish are bred together, all of their offspring show the peculiar reticulated scale pattern. When these fish are bred with common metallic scale fishes, all of the offspring have ordinary metallic scales. When the F_1 generation resulting from this cross is bred together, one quarter of the fish will have the netlike transparent scales, a simple Mendelian factor with a ratio of three to one.

Fish with the netlike transparent scales have the same decoloring characteristics as their siblings, that is, when young they have netlike transparent scales over the gray or wild coloration and gradually turn into orange fish at about the same time as their normal-scaled relatives do. These netlike transparents are never multicolored fish such as the Calicos, but have the same color patterns of red, red and white or all white as Wakins or Ryūkins.

The following charts illustrate the genetic inheritance of guanophores. The pattern holds true irrespective of the presence of pigment cells such as melanophores and xanthophores; the presence of the latter would, of course, determine the color pattern, while the number of guanophores present would determine the degree of transparency.

The following key is used to indicate the degree of guanophore present:

	Appearance		Genetic makeup
	metallic	A high degree of guanophores	ttNN, ttNn
	reticular transparent	Mutation found by Dr Matsui—scales are reticularly transparent	ttnn
	nacreous	Some scales have guanophores and others have none	TtNN, TtNn
	matt or transparent	No guanophores in any parts of the body	TTNN, TTNn, TTnn, Ttnn

The genetic "block" at right illustrates diagramatically the F_2 cross and shows the derivation of the various combinations.

The ratio of matt, nacreous, metallic and reticular transparent is 6:6:3:1.

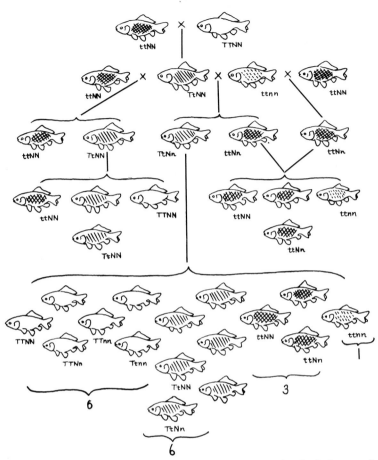

Crossbreeding of a fish with no guanophores and one with a high degree of guanophores.

	TN	Tn	tN	tn
TN	TTNN	TTNn	TtNN	TtNn
Tn	TTNn	TTnn	TtNn	Ttnn
tN	TtNN	TtNn	ttNN	ttNn
tn	TtNn	Ttnn	ttNn	ttnn

Work in England

Some further work on the inheritance of scale transparency has been done by Miss Daphne Morris, a member of the Goldfish Society of Great Britain. Miss Morris, using only one garden pool and a few indoor aquariums, worked with a genetic mutation which was found in a strain of Shubunkins, or Singletails as they are known in England. These closely resemble the fish I have called netlike transparent, and which she has named mock metallic. Her mock metallics were dull-colored fish and did not decolor into orange in the same manner as the fish I was working with, which would seem reasonable since Shubunkins do not decolor.

In breeding her fish together, Miss Morris came up with a type she called pseudo matt. This was transparent-scaled, showing a rich variety of coloration which led some of those familiar with the work done on the netlike transparent fish in Japan and the mock metallic fish in England to conclude that a different mutation was involved; but the American A. F. Tolmer, in a paper presented to the Goldfish Society of Great Britain, has made a strong case that the same factors are involved in both instances.

Looking at the genetic chart, we see four gene combinations which give fish transparent scales: TTNN, TTNn, TTnn, Ttnn. I have grouped all of these fish under the classification of transparent-scale fish. The TTnn differs from the others in having a rich coloration and is the type called pseudo matt.

Fins

Fin characteristics vary with each particular race. The fin with the greatest amount of variation is the caudal fin or tail, which can show up as a single fin, a paired fin, or with any of the variations in between. The ends of the caudal may be round or pointed, deeply forked or square, long or short and grow out of the body at different angles.

The variations in anal fins (which are single in the Crucian Carp) can be single, double or V-shaped in the domestic fish. Dorsal fins may be complete or incomplete, or may be lacking altogether, and all fins can vary in length and shape.

Iron-colored Ribbontail (Tetsuonaga); the color is that of the Crucian Carp.

Heredity of Caudal Fin

Shubunkins, Ryūkins, Orandas and Comets have long tails, while Wakins, Lionheads and Peacock Tails have short tails. When a long-tailed and short-tailed fish are crossed, the tail length of the F_1 generation will be intermediate to the tail length of the parents. If these F_1 fish are bred together, the F_2 generation will have fish with long tails, with short tails and with tails of intermediate length.

It would seem simple enough, then, to assure the breeding of long-tailed fish by simply picking long-tailed parents, but even here a certain amount of selection must come into play and even when breeding with the supposedly "best" parent fish a careful check must be kept on the quality of the fins produced. There is always some tendency for fish to revert to their wild state, even in the purest lines; the caudal fin is, of course, short and single in the wild.

Heredity of Anal Fin

It is to be expected that fish with single caudal fins would have single anal fins, but it is also found that there are single anal fins on fish with paired caudal fins. A single anal fin where there should be double anal fins is considered a defect, and these fish are not used for breeding unless they have other points about them which are exceptional. The tendency to throw single anal fins is stronger, so we can say the single fin is dominant genetically.

Heredity of Dorsal Fin

In the fish which are supposed to be without dorsal fins, any deviation from this norm is considered a serious enough defect to immediately discard the fish. Accordingly, for many generations all of the fish whose standard specifies no dorsal fin, such as Lionheads, have been bred from fish that are completely without any trace of a dorsal. In spite of this, it is not possible to get a line of fish that breeds true for this characteristic. One must still work from the best parent fish and hope for a reasonable amount of young completely lacking the dorsal.

Heredity of Hood

The hood on the Lionhead and the Oranda is definitely an inherited characteristic, but no statistics have ever been compiled on the manner in which this head growth is passed along to the next generation of fish. One difficulty is that while the potential for head growth is passed along genetically, the actual development of the hood depends so much upon the environment in which the fish lives. To be successful in raising fish with good hoods, it is first of all necessary to select the best possible parent stock and then select from among the young fish those with the broadest heads, as the broad-headed fish have the best potential for growing hoods.

A commercial goldfish hatchery must have an ample supply of water of the proper quality and temperature if it is to be successful. This overflow, estimated in excess of 40 million gallons daily, is from just one of five springs at the largest goldfish hatchery in America.

XI Breeding

There is a great deal of pleasure in raising goldfish which have been spawned by others, but it does not compare with the satisfaction of seeing your fish hatch out of the eggs and watching the developing fry, always with the hope that among them there may be the one great champion, the foundation of what hopefully will be a long line of much-admired fish.

Goldfish kept outdoors will spawn readily when the spring comes, but if the eggs are not given the proper attention very few young fish will be raised. On the other hand, if the eggs and young fish are cared for properly, thousands of goldfish can be raised from one spawning.

While it is much easier to induce goldfish to spawn outdoors, with a little care fish will spawn in home aquariums as well.

Aquarium Breeding

Depending upon the size of the fish, breeding goldfish indoors calls for a 20- to 50-gallon tank. If possible the males and females should be separated, preferably in different aquariums, or, if that is not possible, by dividing the aquarium with an opaque partition so that the sexes cannot see each other.

The breeders should be kept between 32° and 45°F for about seven weeks during the latter part of the winter, then gradually raised to between 50° and 60°F for the pre-spawning period and finally to 60° to 70°F in preparation for spawning. Water hyacinths, *Myriophyllum*, Hair grass, other fine floating plants or artificial spawning media may be used to receive the eggs.

Immediately after spawning, remove the parents. Goldfish are capable of producing far more eggs in one spawning than can easily be raised indoors, so unless you have a great deal of tank space in which to spread the young out, don't try to raise them all. If you have outdoor pools in which to raise the fry, you can move the breeders from tank to tank as they spawn and in this way obtain tremendous quantities of eggs. There is a higher percentage of fertilization when goldfish spawn in an aquarium because of the close quarters.

A temperature of about 70°F should be maintained for the eggs and fry. Heavy aeration is desirable; in fact, considering the great number of eggs which are usually laid, it is really mandatory. This aeration should commence even before the eggs hatch.

Thin the fry out when they are about a month old, keeping only the best and disposing of the others.

Conditioning

As spring approaches, it is important that our potential parent fish be in the best possible condition for spawning. Not only will healthy, well-nourished fish spawn more readily, but the quality of their eggs will be better. Well-conditioned parents produce more eggs, a higher percentage of them will be fertile and the fry hatching out will be stronger. As the spawning season approaches, most of the nutriments taken in by the fish go into building up the eggs of the females and the milt of the males. Therefore, pay special attention to feeding parent fish in the early spring. A good supply of live food, such as earthworms, bloodworms, etc., is helpful although not absolutely essential. In addition to its nutritive values, live food accelerates the production of sex cells.

Selecting the Breeders

The quality of the young fish we raise depends in large part on our selecting the best fish for parents. Exceptional breeding fish are not easily obtained, so eventually we find that we must go through hundreds of young fish and cull carefully to find the few fish which we will use to start our own goldfish dynasty.

Goldfish spawn the year after hatching, although occasionally fish which are spawned in the spring and kept under optimum conditions will show signs of being sexually mature in their first autumn. However, fish less than a year old throw few eggs, and these are smaller than those of mature fish. Small eggs hatch out small fry, and this is not desirable. Two- to four-year-old breeders are the best to use.

Fish older than this may spawn a great many large eggs, but often the eggs from these fish past the prime of their spawning abilities are deformed and in large part infertile. It is therefore

Contrasting methods of sorting fish. In Japan, they are selected by hand and sorted into enamel basins; in the USA, a netful of fish is placed on a wet oilcloth or glass-covered table. The pockets in each corner are open and various grades of fish are slipped through each pocket to drop into the water-filled bucket below.

February, when the breeders are selected, is the busiest month in a commercial hatchery. This Red Fantail (female) is about four years old and weighs about one pound.

necessary to select some new fish each year as replacement breeders. It should go without saying that fish which are put aside for breeding purposes should be of known ancestry and outstanding representatives of their variety.

In raising our future breeders, we should give them the best possible care and lots of room, as fish kept in crowded conditions are often reluctant to spawn. Even when we provide more room at breeding time, we often do this too late and then the fish show no inclination to spawn. In some way, whether by hormone secretions or carbon dioxide in the water or some other means, nature seems to prevent overcrowding by advising fish that spawning should not take place under crowded conditions.

Feeding the breeders properly in the autumn is also important if the fish are to be as ready to spawn as we desire the following spring. In the fall they should have more vegetable than animal food. Their food should be of good quality, as well as available in sufficient quantity, and must contain the essential vitamins and minerals so as to enable the breeders to pass the winter in good condition.

Separating the Sexes

As spawning time approaches, it is advisable to separate the males and females so that spawning does not occur before we are ready.

In the square, flat-bottomed concrete pools of Japanese hatcheries, bamboo seines are used to herd the goldfish into a small area from which they are dipped into buckets.

Even when the females are separated from the males, it is a wise precaution not to have any plants or similar objects in the water with them, since these may stimulate the premature ejaculation of eggs, even though no males are present. Naturally, such eggs would be infertile. Separating the males and females for a short while before spawning also seems to increase their interest in each other when they are again placed together.

Depending on the weather, and whether we are spawning the hardier or the more delicate types, we can—in temperate zones such as the Central USA—put them together from late March to early May. If we do this during a spell of nice weather, a spawning of good quality eggs should occur. In the southern USA, spawning cycles will start as early as January or February, but the spawns are light and the fertility low, due probably to the fact that the fish have not gone through a hibernation period.

Conditions Affecting Spawning Time

In addition to the climate, water conditions also have an effect as to when fish will start spawning, since we know, for example, that when fish are kept in water which is overly green from the presence of too much algae, spawning time is likely to be delayed.

The location of the pond also has its influence; spawning will start earlier in a pond which is in a sunny place than it will in a

The public demands fish all year round, so seining goes on even in mid-winter.

pond which is kept shaded. This is because the hormones which control breeding are activated by the lengthening days of spring.

Some people have tried to breed their fish early in the spring or out of season either by putting hormones or other chemicals in the water, or by injecting hormones directly into the fish, or by using heaters to raise the water temperature gradually, or by controlled use of artificial light, or by a combination of these, but generally speaking, artificial inducement to spawning is not recommended. The disruption of the normal yearly cycle may be unsettling to the adult fish, and young fish hatched outside of the normal season seem to be less vigorous than those which are spawned normally. There are additional problems when raising fish in off-seasons, such as providing heat for them and having an adequate supply of natural food available.

Sexing Goldfish

It is extremely difficult to tell the difference between male and female when the fry are less than a year old; however, the females are likely to be bigger than their brothers of the same age. As fish approach their spawning time, it is relatively easy to distinguish the males from the females, although in some of the more highly developed types of fishes, the only sure way to differentiate the sexes is to note which fish lays eggs.

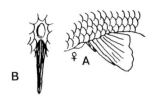

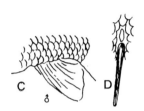

The sex of the mature fish may be determined by the shape and appearance of the anal opening. (A) and (B) show the female in profile and underview, respectively; (C) and (D) show the male. The female's profile is more rounded and, when she is ripe, tends to protrude.

As the eggs mature and develop in the female, a thickening can be noted in her ventral region. At about the same time, the male will start to develop small white tubercles on his gill plates and on the leading rays of his fins, particularly the first ray of the pectoral fin. Excessive growth of tissue on the gill plates of some varieties can make detection of the tubercles difficult, but they can usually be noted on the pectoral fin. To the practiced eye, the anal opening serves to distinguish the sexes (diagram above). The male opening is small and oval, while the female one is larger, projects a little more and is circular in shape. These differences too are most apparent as spawning time approaches, since the female opening will be larger and more distended when the eggs are ripe. When the male is ready for spawning, milt may be pushed out of the ventral opening by running a finger lightly along the sides of the fish. However, when the male is ripe, his tubercles will plainly indicate his sex, and it is not necessary to handle the fish to prove it.

Once spawning is completed, the tubercles may vanish on the male because of decreased sex hormone secretion. As the next spawning time approaches, new tubercles will be seen to appear but on a weaker scale.

Secondary sexual characteristics are most easily distinguished on slender-bodied fish and on those with the normal narrow head.

Courtship

In the spring, when the water temperature has risen to just below

OZARK FISHERIES

Fantails spawning shortly after daybreak. The spawning act is so violent as to disturb the water.

60°F or into the high sixties, you will notice that the goldfish start to group together while swimming about. Small goldfish will follow fish two or three times their size and rub against the larger fish. Soon some of the more active males will single out a female and drive her vigorously through the water. As the actual spawning days draw closer, this driving becomes more prolonged and violent. These are the usual signs which precede the actual spawning, but the more exotic types of fish may not go through these preliminaries, so be warned, if breeding the latter, that there will not necessarily be any preliminary indications.

Spawning commences early in the morning, usually as the first light reaches the pond, and continues to about noon. As the spawning female throws her eggs, other goldfish not in on the spawning drive may follow her about and eat all the eggs they can find. Indeed, once the spawning fishes have completed their activity, they will often turn around and eat the eggs themselves. With such cannibalistic inclinations, a young fish must be fortunate indeed to survive to maturity.

As a rule, spawning starts in April—usually on a fair day following a rainy period. Spawning periods of two to five days are interspersed with rest periods of four to seven days. The first day of spawning usually sees quite a bit of driving, but comparatively few eggs laid; the second and third mornings are usually good; on the fourth morning, spawning actually decreases or ceases.

Weather is a controlling factor. For example, a cold early spring rain on the first or second day will disrupt the spawning. This continues until the water temperatures get up into the eighties, usually in July. The spawning season may be extended through the hottest weather by adding cool water to bring the water temperatures down.

More Males

In spite of all our efforts to select, we sometimes find males which are inactive or halfhearted in their spawning activities; therefore, it is important to provide a surplus of males. The usual proportion is three to one, as extra males seem to insure a high proportion of fertile eggs. Having more males than females in a spawning drive may give the greatest proportion of fertile eggs, but there are times when, for particular reasons, we may want to use a single male and he turns out to be reluctant to spawn. Often, we can still make use of such an inactive male by putting one or two hard-driving males into the spawning pond with him and the female we have chosen. Once the vigorous males start spawning our chosen male will often get the idea, join in and continue to drive even after we have removed the other males. If the reluctant male does not join in the spawning chase, he may still be hand spawned.

The fish gather in the shallow areas, indicating that they are ready to spawn. The nests are on the bank, ready to be put into the pond.   OZARK FISHERIES

The goldfish hatcheries in Kōriyama are famous for the quantity and quality of their goldfishes, which are produced in concrete ponds such as these.

Preparation of the Spawning Pond

To set up a spawning pond, it is only necessary to fill it with good clear water and let it stand in sunshine for several days. The water will then be in proper condition to induce spawning. In commercial fish farms where goldfish are raised by the thousands, the fish are spawned in concrete pools about eight to twelve inches deep. Goldfish seem to spawn earlier in shallow ponds than in deep ones. This is probably due to the greater temperature fluctuation in the shallower water. In early spring a shallow pond can be warmed by one good day of sunshine to a temperature at which the goldfish will spawn. The use of a shallow concrete pond also has another advantage to the commercial breeder, since it is easier to care for and collect the fry in a pond of uniform depth and regular shape.

Spawning Nests

Nests on which the goldfish will spawn can be made up of bunches of fine-leaved water plants such as Anacharis, *Cabomba* or *Myriophyllum* tied together. Water hyacinths are probably the spawning medium most commonly used by the hobbyist. They

A goldfish nest. Spawning material is fastened to wire frames, which are then placed in the shallow areas of the pool.

OZARK FISHERIES

have the advantage of floating naturally while eggs deposited on their trailing roots are easily seen.

It is not necessary to use living plants for fish nests. Clumps of dried willow roots or bunches of Spanish Moss are good substitutes. Nylon mops and nettings, which can be floated by tying them to a piece of wood or cork, are also suitable. Nests made of nonliving materials have an advantage; we can sterilize them by boiling or by chemical means so that we know we are not introducing any pests into our ponds, a danger which is always present when using live plants.

Before putting the fish and the nests in the spawning ponds, any plants or other similar objects on which the fish might spawn should be removed.

Spawning

Goldfish begin spawning when the water reaches about 68°F, but often the fish will not start to spawn until the fish nests are placed in the pond. Rubbing against the nests stimulates the desire to spawn and, for that reason, nests should not be put into a pond beforehand.

Eggs require more oxygen in comparison to volume than do fish; therefore, neither eggs nor nests should rest in the mud or on other debris of organic nature which is decaying, because the

When spawning is completed, the nest is examined to determine the number of eggs. These are clearly visible, like tiny white pearls.

decaying material will use up the oxygen and the eggs will die; nor should they be submerged more than twelve inches, because even though some eggs may hatch in deeper water, many of the fry will not survive the depth.

When selecting the best time for spawning, try to choose a period when the weather is likely to be favorable. If there is a forecast of a cold spell on the way, it would be better to wait, because this time the weatherman may be correct in his prediction. A sudden drop in temperature can delay the hatching of the eggs for several days, and if the chill is severe the young fish can be killed off or so weakened that they never develop properly.

As we said, goldfish usually start to spawn as the first daylight reaches them. One way to collect eggs is to observe the fish each morning to see if they are in a spawning drive and to inspect the fish nests carefully. It is very aggravating when you are dashing off to work in the morning with not a minute to spare and you notice as you hurry by your spawning pond that the eggs which you have been eagerly awaiting are now being laid. If this happens, it is best to remove the nests immediately to a safe place so that the eggs which have already been laid can be saved.

With fish and nests in the spawning pond, we are now ready to collect the eggs. The secret is to collect all our eggs in one day rather than try to collect eggs from several different days' spawnings. One good batch of eggs well cared for will produce more young, and give better results with less trouble, than trying to get several hatches of fry and to bring them all up. If we do gather eggs on different days, however, it should be remembered not to place the different days' spawnings together, since even a few days difference in age at this early stage of a fish's life means that there will be a great difference in the size of the fry, and the fish hatched first might be tempted to eat the fish which hatch later.

When everything is ready, we put the breeders in the spawning pond, along with the nests for collecting the eggs, the morning before we want the spawning to take place. If all goes well, the fish will be depositing eggs on the nests the next morning when we go out to check them. If this happens, we may feel that spawning goldfish is an easy game indeed, but often our fish do not accommodate us by spawning on schedule; for example:

The breeders may not be ready. Either they may not yet be in condition, or they may not be fully mature. Some fish, even though they are old enough and apparently in ready condition, are reluctant to start spawning. Unfortunately, the most reluctant spawners are usually the most highly developed and desirable specimens.

A sudden change in the weather may cause a sudden drop in the water temperature.

Sometimes it appears that fish become nervous in the strange surroundings of the spawning pond, and need a few days to become accustomed to their new quarters.

A change in the general weather pattern also seems to encourage fish to spawn. A long spell of sunny or cloudy weather will often find the fish uninterested in spawning until the weather pattern changes.

Just as the change in weather often wakens the spawning impulse in our fish, a partial change of water may have the same effect. The usual precautions necessary when making a change of water should be observed; otherwise we may shock the fish and delay spawning even further, or if we do a really bad job, we might kill the breeders.

We know that many conditions, such as moon phase, barometer readings, relation between air temperature and water temperature and water chemistry affect goldfish spawning; unfortunately, as yet no complete findings have been set down as to how important each of these is and how they might interact with each other. The

Goldfish Society of Great Britain has been attempting to keep records, and perhaps one day enough data will be available for us to tell when our fish are most likely to spawn.

One morning—whether it is the time we have chosen or not—we will discover that our fish are spawning. A natural tendency is to let them continue until they have finished laying the last egg, which is usually about noon. It is not necessary, however, to collect every last possible egg unless obtaining sheer numbers of fish is our goal. Indeed, some fanciers strongly believe that the first eggs spawned are the best ones, and collect only those eggs which have been laid in the first hour or two. Often one female will throw 4,000 to 5,000 eggs, and we might just as well work with half that number, especially if we have the better half.

The eggs are adhesive and will stick to just about anything. They are about 1.5 mm in diameter, the size of a pinhead, but as they take on water they increase in size. After two or three hours, the eggs are water-hardened and if kept at 50° to 55°F they can at this stage be transported safely for long distances.

If we do not remove the first nests before the spawning is completed, we should do so just as soon as we see that the fish are no longer interested in laying eggs, because they will soon turn around and eat them.

Hatching

Sometimes it is more convenient, once spawning is completed, to remove the adult fish. A greater number of eggs will hatch using this method, since it is never possible for the spawning nests to catch all of the eggs, because some may fall to the bottom while others adhere to the pond sides. Usually, however, we find it more practical to transfer the nests to a hatching pond.

Before transferring the nests, we must make sure that the water temperature is the same in the hatching pond as in the spawning pond. Even after the eggs are put into the hatching pond, they should be protected against sudden temperature changes which might come about from a heavy rain or from a drastic difference between the daytime and the nighttime temperatures. If the hatching pond is shaded somewhat from direct sunlight, the daily temperature variation will not be as drastic. Rattan blinds or bamboo covers can be used as protection against too much sun.

Fish are placed in these "graders" to be separated according to size. The smaller fish swim out between the bars; the larger are ready for sale.

An opaque plastic cover can be used to shade the water, and it will also serve the double purpose of protection from a particularly heavy fall of rain. The water should be clean, with a minimum of organic matter in it, as decomposition will deplete the oxygen.

At a water temperature of about 68°F, goldfish eggs normally hatch in four or five days. It is possible to distinguish quickly between the fertile and infertile eggs, as the day after spawning the infertile ones will be opaque, while the fertile eggs, which can vary in color from a pale amber to a rather pale yellow, will remain clear. About two days later, the dead eggs will often start to look fuzzy as fungus develops on them, while we should be able to see the eyes of the fish formed inside the fertile eggs. It is probably true that the shorter the hatching time, the less danger that the fungus will spread to the live eggs. One way to control the fungus is to soak the fish nests in a malachite green solution of from one part malachite green to 500,000 parts water (see chapter on Diseases) to one part to 1,000,000 for about fifteen minutes. The hatching time is directly related to the water temperature, taking about six days at 56°F and about two days at 80°F. A hatching time of four to five days is ideal; if the hatching period is either lengthened or shortened the health and quality of the young fish is adversely affected.

This seine is used at a commercial goldfish hatchery in the USA. It is 150 feet long by 8 feet deep, with a ⅜-inch mesh. This haul contained about 560 pounds, dry weight, of Fantails, between 80–85,000 fish.

Maturation

The rate of maturation is affected by the temperature. At 68°F they become "eyed," that is the eyes of the fry start to appear inside the eggs, about three days after they are laid. At this stage it is safe to move them. Two days later, the fry will start to work their way out of the transparent shell. If the eggs are kept at high temperatures they will start hatching in less than five days; hatching will be prolonged if eggs are kept at lower temperatures. Neither of the extremes is favorable and it is best if fish are hatched out in their normal time at moderate temperatures.

At the time of hatching, the fry are about five mm in length (less than ¼-inch). The eggs open up like chestnut burrs to release the young fish. The fry still have the yolk attached, which can be seen as a sac attached to their bellies. This will nourish them for the first few days.

They are able to jerk about in the water, but cannot sustain the swimming motion and spend most of their time resting on the bottom or hanging on the sides of the pond or on some flat plant. In two or three days, as the yolk sac becomes absorbed, the fry start to swim about, searching for food which at this stage consists mainly of microscopic or semi-microscopic animalcules or zoöplankton. At this early stage of development, the fry are very delicate and should not be moved or netted. A sudden change of temperature, or even a heavy rainfall, can kill all or most of them.

A month after hatching, the fry start to look like goldfish and their covering of scales can be seen clearly. In the fish that go through the color-fading-away change, the lightening of color soon starts, and if the strain is one which decolors quickly, the wild color can be completely gone in another week to ten days.

By the fall the fry are considered adult fish. They will spend the winter resting and preparing to become parents themselves the next spring.

Feeding the Fry

Young fish given a good start in life will be healthy, well-developed adults, but if feeding is neglected in the first week, so that they get improper food or only enough food to survive, development is irreparably retarded.

As soon as the fry start to swim, they should be given all that they can eat of newly hatched brine shrimp, finely sieved *Daphnia* or other minute animals lumped together under the popular name of "infusoria." Another excellent food for newly hatched goldfish is the hardboiled yolk of an egg squeezed through fine cloth and then stirred throughly into a small amount of water. The solution of egg yolk and water can then be spread among the young fish. Dried powedered egg yolk can be used, and it has the advantage of mixing readily.

Some of the methods used commercially will not work out too

These slat covered boxes have wire bottoms both for sanitation and circulation. Fish are conditioned for shipment by being held in cold running water for several days to a week. They are fed lightly if at all.

well for the home breeder, because when raising goldfish at home there is not nearly as much water volume, and the water quality can deteriorate quickly from a small amount of uneaten food.

At home, as on a fish farm, finely sieved *Daphnia* is the best food for starting the young fry off right in life; but not too many of us are lucky enough to have access to a good *Daphnia* supply these days, and if we use egg yolk we must be careful, since an excess of this food can cause the water to pollute. Fortunately, newly hatched brine shrimp is an excellent food for fry just starting to eat, and although they might be somewhat expensive in a large-scale operation, they will be found to be well worth their cost for the several weeks they are necessary. Even fish just out of the egg can eat the freshly hatched brine shrimp or *nauplii*, and it is one of the foods least likely to spoil the water. In two or three weeks the brine shrimp diet can be supplemented by some of the dried foods which are sold in pet stores. If cared for properly, the young fishes should be about $\frac{1}{2}$-inch long at the end of six weeks. The fry will grow remarkably fast if the water is always kept very light green in color, either by means of controlling the amount of light or by draining off and adding water. If the algae spores are present, partial changes of water will stimulate their growth.

During these early stages, the fry can be fed many times a day—but watch the quantities. If there should be a sudden halt in the growth of the fish accompanied by a decreased appetite, it would indicate that the population is starting to outgrow its surroundings and that the water condition may be entering a dangerous phase. At this time we should be ready to spread the fish out into other ponds or tanks, and we should also start thinning out the fish by disposing of those we do not intend to keep so that more room and care can be given to the others.

On the commercial Japanese fish farms, the usual method of feeding the young fish to produce maximum growth is to put them into specially prepared ponds in which *Daphnia* are flourishing. The fish are watched closely and as they exhaust the supply of *Daphnia* in one pond, they are transferred to another where a good *Daphnia* culture is flourishing. The fry grow so fast under these conditions that they will soon outstrip the supply of *Daphnia* ponds, and the *Daphnia* should be supplemented with other foods. A mixture of fish meal, rice bran, wheat flour and various millet by-products are boiled together and formed into a dumpling shape. The fish farmer can either make up his own mixture, or buy a commercial fish food mixture and either grind it very fine or mix it with hot water to make a paste which the young fish can peck on.

A home breeder can make up his own paste food by adding to boiling water a mixture of oatmeal and dried ground shrimp with the yolk of an egg stirred in. If refrigerated this will keep for several days. A small lump placed in a dish in the tank will maintain its freshness for a day.

The paste food is placed in dishes which are suspended at a depth of about eight inches every six feet or so along the side of the pond. The young fish soon become accustomed to these feeding stations, and the fish farmer has a chance to observe his fish and determine whether he is putting out the right amount of food. Enough food is put into these dishes so that they only have to be filled once each day. Uneaten excess should be removed.

Daphnia Ponds

Where large numbers of goldfish are being planned, such as in a commercial hatchery, one step usually taken before the fish are allowed to spawn is the preparation of the *Daphnia* ponds. In the Nara district of Japan, there are many natural ponds which produce *Daphnia*, and the goldfish hatcheries gather these crustaceans which are unexcelled as a food for the young fish. The problem is that, in these natural ponds, one day the water is teeming with millions of the little water fleas, and the next they mysteriously disappear. Since a hatchery cannot rely on the un-certain supply of *Daphnia* that can be taken from a wild pond, the bulk must be raised in specially prepared ponds. Fertilizers, either organic or inorganic (or combinations of both), are used for the propagation of *Daphnia*. Such fertilizers as cattle and chicken manure, fish meal, silk worm chrysalides, soya bean sauce lees and rice bran are all excellent for preparation of the *Daphnia* pond. However, some of these are not too pleasant to handle.

To prepare a *Daphnia* pond: drain the pond during the winter and sprinkle the bottom with lime to accelerate the decomposition of the organic matter on the pond bottom; spread manure or other fertilizer on the pond bottom and introduce a little water in

Hi-cap, or Goosehead Oranda, a Chinese variety with the cranial portion developed to form a cap.

the pond at this time in order to distribute the fertilizer evenly; fill the pond with water at the end of winter so that the fertilizer may start the growth of bacteria in the water. The water will soon be full of protozoans and other phytoplankton which are the natural food of *Daphnia*. The *Daphnia* winter eggs are now ready to hatch out into the water of the pond, which has become deep green from the heavy fertilization. If these steps are taken, the pond will soon be swarming with *Daphnia*.

Culling

If the young fish have been fed properly they will be about ¼-inch long about two weeks after hatching. At this early stage, we are ready to start culling out and separating.

If there are any real secrets to raising champion goldfish, early selective culling is one of the most important. It is difficult to persuade a fancier who has bred fish for the first time to start discarding some of his fish because they have undesirable characteristics. Successful breeders of the more select varieties are called ruthless cullers, but since ruthlessness implies a lack of feeling, "highly selective" would be a better term. It is impossible for most of us to raise all of the fish hatched from even one spawning to maturity, but the less crowded a brood of young fish is, the less likely they are to fall prey to disease or to succumb to foul water. If young fish are crowded, it is a common story to find them in good health one day and dying off the next. Usually a disease of the gills, such as fluke (*Dactylogyrus*) infestation, will be the cause. Unfortunately, by the time the first fish succumb, the disease—

encouraged by crowding—has reached epidemic proportions, and the fry are all infected and will die off in a day or two.

It is much better to select several of the better young fish as early as possible and rear them carefully. It is a great satisfaction to watch young fish grow and develop properly, but very frustrating to see a brood struggle just to keep alive.

If it is best to cull goldfish as early as possible, just how early can one start? It depends on the expertise of the person doing the selecting. One of the more successful breeders of Veiltails starts to cull his fish when they are only three to four days old, by using a jeweler's loupe to examine them. At this stage, fish can only be examined for more obvious defects, such as those showing webbed caudal fins. In May, this breeder might have 1,000 fry; in June, 500; in July, 250; in August, 100; in September, 25 and by October, a dozen might be all that have survived the weeding process. The point is that these dozen left are the fish that the breeder has selected, and not those which have been the lucky survivors. These methods of culling have been proved over the years. First the larger fry should be separated, since they will soon start to monopolize the food and, very often, start eating their smaller brothers and sisters as well. Then those fish which show obvious deformities and undesirable characteristics, such as a single tail where they should have a double tail, should be discarded.

One might object that if culling is started too early there is always the risk of making a mistake and discarding a good fish, but this risk is far outweighed by the troubles which are certain to come if one attempts to keep more fish than can be properly managed. (If there were sufficient resources available to a fancier where young fish could be spread out in larger quarters as they grew, so that all of the fish could be examined at the end of the

A shallow net is used for catching the valuable species, as the deeper bag might damage the scales. This is a female Lionhead, swollen with roe.

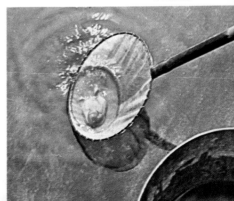

year—or, better still, at the end of two years—it must be admitted that this would be the ideal way to raise and select the best possible fish).

Therefore, the more ponds and containers at our disposal, the better our chances are.

The question then might be asked, what chance does the fancier with a few tanks in the home have of breeding and raising goldfish? To be sure, outdoor pools are a distinct help in keeping goldfish, but the disadvantage of having to raise goldfish in tanks can at times be turned into an advantage because the breeder who works indoors with only a few tanks is forced to adopt from the very beginning good feeding and housekeeping habits.

Culling Ranchū

Since the premier goldfish is the Ranchū or Lionhead, we might use him as an example of the work that goes into selecting a fish of the first magnitude.

The shape of the caudal fin is one of the first things for which Ranchū fry are examined. Even among broods which are hatched

This pair of Orandas is beautiful to look at, but they are not of show or breeding quality. The well-developed hoods hardly compensate for the lack of depth in the body and the irregularities of the tail.

from selected parents of known ancestry, some of these young fish will have a single caudal fin like the ancestral Crucian Carp. Others have ends which overlap in the center; some have T-shaped tails which form too wide an opening and there are the intermediate shapes such as the triple or cherry blossom type. All of these are discarded.

With the remaining fish, the second feature to examine is the back, or dorsal, area. Even in very young fish it is easy to pick out those with normal dorsal fins or those with vestiges of a dorsal fin which are called masts or spikes. Fish showing these features are discarded. As the fry grow somewhat larger, imperfections on the back now start to show up, such as fish with straight backs, hollow backs or any kinds of bumps or unevenness. The back should rise in a smooth curve, be free of any imperfections and when viewed from above should be broad.

The region about the caudal peduncle is the third area which must be closely examined. The width of the dorsal area and the breadth of the caudal peduncle should be in proportion to each other, and smoothly match at the rear of the dorsal area where they join. Fish with a broad back and a thickened caudal peduncle are deemed to be superior Ranchūs.

So far we have not even mentioned the one feature of the Ranchū which distinguishes it, and that is the hood or lion-headed growth. In the early stages, while we are selecting for the features mentioned above, it is not really possible to tell which of our fish are going to develop the biggest hood. One indication of potential for good hood growth is a head which is large and broad when viewed from above, since we know that fish with broad heads have the best potential. As mentioned previously, environment and diet play a large part in the eventual development of the Ranchū head.

After we have gone through all of this labor in selecting and raising young fish, as they mature they will, unfortunately, at times develop characteristics contrary to our expectations and desires. On the other hand, a fish with a few minor defects may develop into an unexpectedly good specimen. Such are the joys and griefs of the Ranchū fancier.

Even when our young Ranchus meet all of the standards for body conformity and fin shape, we still have to worry about whether they are going to develop the beautiful coloring which will enhance their perfection of shape. Should they achieve the colors we are looking for, we still must wonder whether they will carry themselves regally when swimming about and resting. These are all fine points which the critical judges will consider at the Ranchū competitions.

The raising of superior Ranchūs is, as we can see, not an easy task, but its very difficulty is the thing that most commends it to the fancier. The professional breeders generally find the Ranchū requires too much time and effort to be commercially profitable and worthy of their attention, but the amateur fanciers lovingly care for their Ranchūs so that they may be admired by all.

The Lionhead Caudal—Points to Consider

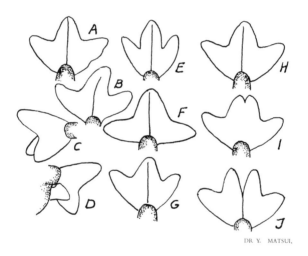

DR Y. MATSUI.

A — Shortened
B — Wry or twisted
C — Too narrow (profile)
D — Protruding anal fin
E — Too narrow (top view)
F — Too open
G — Asymmetrical
H, I and J — Three acceptable types

Faults Commonly Seen in Lionheads

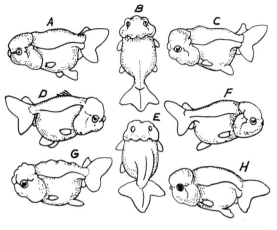

DR. Y. MATSUI

A — Indented back
B — Caudal peduncle overlength
C — Humpback
D — Vestigal dorsal fin
E — Crooked back
F — Beeline-back rises too much
G — Broken back line
H — Bent back

A Matter of Pride

It is no wonder, then, that fish which reach championship status at the national shows are priced at hundreds and even thousands of dollars. Further, even though these vast sums are offered, the proud owners seldom part with a fish which represents so much time, patience and years of hopeful anticipation. Not only does the owner want to hold onto the fish into which so much of himself has gone, but he is also hoping that his champion can pass the winning characteristics on to future generations.

A little ingenuity and a lot of imagination created this lovely garden setting, The pool is made of a sheet of heavy plastic edged with brick.

XII   Garden Pools

By far the best place for a fancier to keep goldfish is outdoors, and for most of us this means a garden pool. The pool should be as large as practical and in an open and airy location. It should be set up where it will not get too much shade or it will not receive adequate sunlight during the spring, fall and winter. This is important, because unless sunlight reaches the pond directly, the goldfish growth will be retarded and the spring spawning is likely to be late. During the summer there may be too much hot, direct sunlight on a pond, but then we can always shade the pond with screens or other covers. We should also try to keep our ponds away from trees or shrubbery. These may not only give more shade than is desirable, but the run-off of rain water from certain leaves may be toxic and the leaves themselves, falling into the pond, may foul the water before we realize it.

Plan Your Pool

It would also be helpful if we could pick a high spot, as this will make it easier to drain the pool. After we have decided on the location, the next step is to make a sketch of the layout of the pool, including details of the most practical arrangement of the drainpipes.

Those of us who have kept goldfish indoors are always pleasantly surprised to see how the move to an outdoor pool perks up the fish, how their growth accelerates and how their colors deepen and become more vivid. In garden pools, goldfish require less care than when they are kept indoors. During the winter, if the pond is not crowded, no water changes are necessary. In the spring and fall, when water temperatures are low, water changing can be kept to a minimum, since the fish are feeding less in the cooler temperatures and consuming less oxygen. Often all that is required for pool maintenance from fall to spring is replacement of the water lost by evaporation.

Predators

There are many sizes and shapes of garden pools. If one just wants to keep a few goldfish as a decorative addition to the garden, a single pool is adequate. With this lone pool we have to decide whether we are designing a pool solely for its aesthetic place in our garden, or whether its main function is as a home for goldfish. If we build a pool with irregularly shaped walls of stones and rocks, it is pleasing in appearance, but it may be difficult to cover the pool for protection from cats or other predators. Goldfish which have been tamed by regular feedings are easy prey for the fish-hunting cat, and may even gather at the spot where a paw brushes the water. If goldfish are kept in an unprotected pool, they should be the faster varieties such as Wakin or Comet, and even then we should be prepared to lose an occasional fish. Assuming that most who read this book do not consider their goldfish as incidental ornaments to the garden pool, a square or rectangular shaped pond will be best.

Several If Possible

For those who are going to enjoy the complete cycle of raising, spawning and growing young fish, it would be desirable to have three or more pools. If more than one variety is kept, they must be separated at spawning time or a lot of time may be wasted caring for fry of uncertain lineage. Even if we keep only one variety of goldfish, spare ponds in which to place fish when we are changing water or to separate fish at breeding time or to isolate sick fish make fishkeeping easier and less troublesome.

When we have a multi-pool arrangement, the pools should be grouped so that the filling and draining is convenient. If water changing is an onerous task, it is inevitable that this job will be neglected or done only when the water quality becomes so bad that we must rescue our fish or lose them. If we can easily drain down our ponds and fill them, we are more likely to maintain a regular schedule. Keeping goldfish should be a pleasure which does not require too much time. The story of the fishkeeper who abandons his hobby because he finds an unreasonable amount of time is demanded to care for his fish has been repeated all too often.

Construction of Garden Pools

Digging and disposal of earth can be minimized somewhat if we keep our pools above ground level, but if we expect to use our pools throughout the year, this is suitable only where the winter climate is not severe enough to put more than a thin film of ice on the water. We have only to think of the damage that can be done to an unprotected automobile engine which freezes up in the winter to realize that a heavy freeze can rupture the walls of the pool due to the tremendous pressure exerted by the ice. If a pond is to be suitable for keeping fish over the winter, it not only must be set below ground level, it must also extend below the frost line. In some multi-pond arrangements, often only one or two of the ponds are made deep enough to winter fish.

At one time, the usual way to construct a pond was to pour concrete into wooden frames. This makes a strong pond, and if we remember the cardinal rule which is to pour all the concrete for the walls at one time, it also makes a leak-free pool. Mixing and pouring concrete is hard work, and there is always the temptation to postpone completing the job, but that is poor policy. When layers of concrete are poured on different days, minute seams are formed and these are a constant invitation to leaks. The preferred proportion is one part cement, two parts

The eyes of the Celestial Goldfish should look straight up. Surprisingly enough, although they always look towards heaven, they do not need any more protection from the sun than do more normal-eyed goldfish.

A duck's-eye view of goldfish in the pool. Mallards, even females like this one, will eat small fish.

sand, three parts coarse aggregate (gravel). The wall thickness should be four to six inches, with the bottom at least six inches.

A somewhat easier method of pond construction is to use waterproof concrete blocks which are available in different sizes and proportions. The holes should be filled with concrete to prevent their filling with water, as this may freeze during severe weather and split the block.

In a pond made of block construction, the bottom should be of poured concrete with a slight slope toward the drain. A good drain outlet can be made from a bathtub outlet, obtainable in hardware stores. An overflow pipe with a screen should be set in this to prevent the pool from overflowing during a heavy rain. A stand-pipe serves another purpose; by putting a hose down to the bottom and allowing the water to run slowly, you can partially change or freshen the pool. This is particularly desirable during the hot summer months. After the poured concrete bottom of the pond has hardened, concrete blocks are then used to make the walls, leaving a space of about one inch between the inside of the block and the earthwall of the excavation. The blocks are laid with mortar, and when they have dried for several days, concrete should be poured into the space between the blocks and the earthwall. Here too the concrete should be poured in a single operation to give maximum strength and watertightness.

Whether the pond is of solid or of block construction, a finishing coat of cement is laid—available from masonry suppliers or paint stores in various colors—and should be brushed over the inside of the pond to seal any minute cracks and to give it a dense surface finish. This finishing coat should not be allowed to dry out too quickly, or the cement will not cure properly. Cover it with sheets of newspaper or burlap kept damp with a sprinkling of water for a day or more to help the cement harden properly. The pond should be shaded from direct sunlight while the cement is setting.

A good homemade cement paint can be made by mixing port-land cement and water to the consistency of a thin paste, suitable for brushing.

If the pond lip is set at ground level, there should be a six to eight inch wall around the pond to keep mud from washing in. If the pond is not supplied with a standpipe drain, a few screened overflow holes should be set just above ground level.

The size of the pool depends on one's ambition and the space available. Medium-sized ponds are generally more satisfactory than very large or very small ones. A good average size would be a pond from $4\frac{1}{2}$ to 10 feet square. A depth of eight to ten inches is sufficient in milder climates as fish can winter in these if they are covered during the coldest weather; but in colder climates a pond with a depth of up to $2\frac{1}{2}$ feet below ground level may be necessary for wintering fish. If you call your local weather bureau, they will be glad to give you the maximum frost depth for your area.

Winter Care

Pools set below ground level should not be drained during the winter, as the ground freezing will exert pressure inwards. The outward sloping walls will permit the water within the pond to expand upwards. Some pools, rather than sloping from bottom to top, have the walls vertical two thirds of the way up from the bottom, then flare outwards.

An old trick to prevent ice damage is to place a five-gallon pail in the pool half filled with rocks so that it floats partially submerged, or suspended with wire in the center of the pond; it should be sealed so that water cannot enter. The ice pressure will crush the empty bucket, thus relieving the outward pressure.

If you cover the pond, use a clear plastic and keep the ice and snow brushed off, so that light can penetrate.

Curing the Concrete

Goldfish cannot be released into the newly constructed pond until the highly alkaline effects of the new concrete have been neutralized. Fill the pond with water and allow it to stand for two weeks; several changes of water will usually wash away the free alkali. Brushing the sides of the pond with vinegar will also help. Before stocking with fish, it is a precaution to put one or two less valuable fish in the pond and see if they survive for a week or so.

Plastic Ponds

For many years ponds of poured concrete or block construction

This female Oranda is about one year old and shows excellent development.

were the only types of garden pools, but today the versatility of various plastic materials provides other alternatives. Reinforced fiberglass is probably the sturdiest of the new materials. Pools made of this material can be kept above ground or buried, and will give many years of service. There are several types of inexpensive plastic children's wading pools and these make good homes for goldfish, but because of the relatively soft walls, it is not recommended that they be used for below-ground-level pools. Some plastics are toxic to fish, so best check with the manufacturer first, or if that is not possible try a few inexpensive fish first.

Plastic Sheets

Sheets of plastic up to 40 feet wide are sold which can be used to line excavations in the ground. The walls of these excavations should be sloping inward, and any sharp rocks or other objects which might puncture the plastic should be eliminated before the sheeting is laid over the pond bottom and sides. This type of construction has been used by farmers to water their cattle or to make a pond for swimming, and has proven to be safe and inexpensive. Stones or bricks can be used to build a wall around the pond.

Plastic sheeting can also be used in making above-ground ponds and tanks. A wooden box lined with plastic makes a very satisfactory tank and requires no great construction skill. Plastic sheeting used for pond construction is usually black, since black resists deterioration from sunlight better than clear sheeting does. Clear plastic, however, is available and the clear plastic may be hung in a wooden frame, thus giving us an opportunity to view the fish from the side.

In discussing the construction of concrete or block ponds, we mentioned the importance of a proper drainage system. However, for the plastic pools we need another system to empty our ponds. The simplest way is to siphon off the water, if there is an area available which is lower than the lowest level of our pool where we can drop the outlet end of the siphon; so again we see the importance of picking a high spot for the pool.

Inexpensive pumps are also available to drain pools. Cellar sump pumps are effective; they can also be used as aerators and

The goldfish pond need not be strictly functional. Fiberglass rocks can be substituted for natural ones, and pockets of earth left between to hold masses of flowering annuals.

recirculators. Siphoning or pumping will eliminate the necessity for constructing a drainage system. Not only will the labor of constructing a drainage system be saved, but since the area around drain outlets is prone to leaks, the absence of drain outlets means one thing less to worry about.

The last and most important item to consider in setting up our pond is to see that it is adequately fenced, as an inquisitive child can topple into a pond and drown. Prevention of such a tragedy is the responsibility of the fishkeeper. Where a pond location does not permit fencing, a stout cover must be placed over the pond. Ideally, the cover should be made of wire mesh which is heavy enough to support the weight of a child, and the cover should be heavy enough or fastened in some manner so that young children cannot remove it.

Computing Capacity

To compute the gallon capacity of a rectangular tank, multiply the length (feet) by the width (feet) by the average depth (feet) by 7.5 (for English gallons the last figure should be 6.25).

To compute the gallon capacity of a circular pool, multiply the depth (feet) by the diameter squared (feet) by 5.9 (for English gallons the last figure should be 4.9).

Biological Pond Filter

Most fishkeepers can see the advantage of a filter in the aquarium context, but not everyone appreciates their use and value with small ponds. It is surprising how uncomplicated a pond filter can be, using just a straightforward $\frac{1}{2}$-inch capacity water pump. All that is needed is a chamber situated just above water level, filled with activated charcoal or hard burnt clinker (hard residue of burned coal) of uniform size—about one inch in diameter.

Spray the water over the clinker and allow it to run back into the pond over a very shallow dam. This will not only filter out the impurities, but reoxygenate the water. The "slimy-to-the-touch" film which forms on the clinker is a complex zoogleal film made up of animal and plant life which feeds and thrives on the organic matter which ordinarily pollutes water. Once established, a filter can run without any bother and a minimum of attention, sometimes for several years.

Spring and fall the film will slough off from the clinker to make way for a new growth and, at this time, take out the clinker, wash it under the tap and replace.

Water clarity is obtained not by a fine pore filter but by reducing the turbulence of the water to allow the larger particles to sink to the bottom of the filter and settle, while the finer particles—usually bacterial colonies—are consumed as food by the zoogleal film. If the filter chamber is above the water level, the efficiency is high, but the flow of water must be continuous, for if the clinker dries out the biological life will die off. If the filter chamber is submerged, the efficiency is reduced but it is still good enough for fishkeeping purposes, and, of course, as long as it is submerged there is no danger of its drying out.

Goldfish Calendars

Goldfish are creatures whose activities are greatly affected by seasonal changes. When kept in garden pools in the temperate zone throughout the year, goldfish will go through the same life cycles as do their relatives in natural bodies of water.

January and February

During the cold days in the dead of winter, goldfish will group together in a corner of the pond and remain so quiet that it seems that they are not even breathing. Even at this time of year, it is important that some sunlight reach our fish, and on a clear sunny day it is advisable to expose the pond to the air and sunlight. A good way to keep an area open is to hang a 25- to 50-watt waterproof aquarium heater just below the surface. This can be turned on to melt the ice before it forms a thick sheet.

Any disturbances during this dormant period should be avoided, since they tend to increase the metabolism and cause the fish to consume precious food reserves.

We should not feed our fish while they are dormant. They can pass the winter nicely by drawing on the nutrients which they have been storing in their bodies during the warm weather. If goldfish are fed during the winter, their digestive systems may not be able to handle the foods we give them, since their bodily functions are slowed down. A greater danger is that they will leave the proffered food and that it will foul the water.

Where winters are mild, we may notice our fish seeking food even in January and February. Careful feedings of *Daphnia* might be tried, since uneaten *Daphnia* which continue to swim about will not foul the water. It must be remembered, however, that in the limited area of the garden pool the *Daphnia* are competing with the goldfish for the available oxygen.

Leaving the fish alone may be the best thing we can do for them. When there is a heavy loss of fish in the winter, the trouble almost always can be traced to overcrowding or to pools which were not properly cleaned before the dormant period.

RICHARD LAW

An adult male Oranda. The excessive length of its body may be due to its having been raised in a pool. Tank-raised fishes of this type are fed more heavily, which usually results in the body being deeper.

March

During March, the goldfish will start swimming slowly about and gather toward the surface where the sun first warms the water.

Not having eaten during the winter, they will have lost up to 10 to 20 per cent of their weight. Our natural inclination might be to start feeding heavily to make up for the winter weight loss, but we must remember that our fish are still weak in March and not able to handle a heavy diet. The operation of their digestive juices is related to the temperature, so it is best to feed them sparingly with small quantities of live food. If we resort to prepared foods, it is best that this be some type of boiled or paste food which is light and easily digested. Do not be in any hurry to increase the quantities of food until the activity and appetite of the fish clearly indicate that they are ready.

If a covering has protected the pool during the winter, it should be removed in late March, and it is important that this be done on a cloudless day.

April and May

In these months the activity and appetite of the goldfish becomes greater and the 2-year-old fish will be spawning. As the temperature and hours of daylight increase, the pond water will start to turn green and water changing in the pool begins. Early in the season there will be days when the temperature will drop sharply, or when evenings are quite cold after the sun goes down, and it is well to cover our pools at these times to protect the fish from sudden temperature changes.

June

In Japan, the sultry rainy season sets in about mid-June. At this time goldfish often seem to be affected by the unpleasant weather and swim about dispiritedly. When this happens, the amount of food should be reduced until they perk up again.

During unsettled weather it is necessary to be particularly careful when changing water. In fact, if the water is in fairly good condition, we should avoid making any change. If we must change all or part of the water, we should do so when there is a lull in the rain and be sure to return some of the old water after it has been strained through a cloth. From early spring until after the rainy season, we should always return a certain amount of the old green water to the pond along with clear, fresh water.

July and August

In Japan, early in July the rainy season is over and the weather turns very hot. The pool, if left untended, would get so green that we could not even see the fish. Dark green water is dangerous for our fish, so the need for water management is especially pressing in these hot sunny days. Pools should be at least partially covered with well-insulated bamboo blinds or fiberglass slats or similar screening. This will help moderate the water temperature by keeping the heat of the sun off the pool, and it will also slow down the growth of the green algae by reducing the light.

The rise of temperature at this time of year and the increased activity of the fish give them voracious appetites, and these are the months where the growth of our fish is most rapid. In very hot weather, however, we will notice that our fish are not always interested in feeding during the heat of the day when the water temperatures are at their height. We must feed them early in the morning or in the cool of the evening. Here we can take a clue from the fishermen who in summer make their best catches at dawn or in the hours just before darkness.

September and October

These are the last months in which goldfish will continue to grow. Late in the autumn when the cold winds begin to blow and the water starts to cool down, we will notice the activity of our fish decrease. Their need for food will diminish; therefore, we should start cutting down their rations. By the end of October, light feeding once a day is all that our fish should be getting.

Again, care must be taken when changing water at this time of year and the fish should be treated gently.

November and December

In November, goldfish stop eating almost completely. They can be fed once or twice a week, and carefully observed to see that they are still interested in the food. By the end of November, feeding should be discontinued altogether.

The wintering pond should be as clean as possible and the cover placed over the pool to keep the water from freezing. I believe that a freeze can adversely affect fish, although in nature ice does form over the goldfish. There is a school of thought which holds that these conditions ought to be duplicated in our garden pools.

My objection is that while the Crucian Carp does live very well under a thick covering of ice, some of our domesticated varieties of goldfish are far less hardy. One thing is certain: no matter what variety of fish we attempt to winter outdoors, their ability to survive the winter depends in great measure on the care we have given them during the year to build up their strength.

It might be well to bring at least some of the specially valued fish indoors in October if facilities are available. They should be brought in, in the water from the pool in which they have been living, and we should make the temperature transition from outdoors to indoors as gradual as possible. When fish are brought indoors in October, they may spawn any time shortly thereafter, although the most likely time for indoor spawning is from February to April.

XIII   Water Lilies

The following instructions for planting and caring for Water lilies are printed by courtesy of William Tricker, Inc.

How to Plant

Water lilies are very easy to grow. Under natural conditions the roots are in rich soil in the shallow water of a marsh or pond exposed to full sunshine. These conditions are easily reproduced in the garden. In natural ponds, hardy Water lilies may be planted in water from 6 to 18 inches deep and are planted simply by pressing the root into the good soil at the bottom. Small artificial pools should be at least one foot deep, allowing for six inches of water over six inches of soil. In larger pools we always recommend the use of containers, either tubs or boxes, holding at least one bushel of soil. The depth of the water may be from six to twelve inches over the tub or container. Artificial ponds need not be more than 24 inches deep. Twenty inches makes a satisfactory depth. Medium sized tubs are excellent for Water lilies in pools. It is best to provide a separate container for each Water lily or Lotus.

These pictures of some of the more representative and hardy of the always popular Water lilies were provided by Slocum Water Gardens, Winter Haven, Florida. These are divided into three groups: day-blooming tropical, night-blooming tropical and hardy. There are also representatives of the less common

Day-blooming tropical lily—Yellow Dazzler. The butterfly which landed just as the picture was snapped is a Black Swallowtail.

Day-blooming tropical lily—King of Blues. This variety was introduced by Slocum Water Gardens.

Night-blooming tropical lily — Maroon Beauty, introduced by Perry D. Slocum.

Night-blooming tropical lily—Red Flare, with reddish purple leaves.

Lotus and Victoria Lily. Of all the groups, only the hardy Water lilies can be termed truly "hardy," as we understand the term. However, the representatives of the other groups have been selected as being hardy for their type.

Hardy Water lily — Attraction, a large, blood-red, hardy Water lily with white sepals.

Hardy Water lily—Gonnere, also known as Snowball.

Hardy Water lily—Sunrise, the largest of the hardy Water lilies.

Hardy Water lily—Comanche, a changeable orange. This lily is still in full bloom even though it is so late in the season that the autumn leaves have begun to fall.

Hardy Water lily—Rose Arey, a lovely cerise pink.

Lotus lily. A close-up of an improved type of Egyptian Lotus, showing the seed pod. Pink with a yellow center.

Victoria lily. The pads of these lilies are so large that they support a full-grown model, as shown here.

A garden pool made from an old tub, planted with Gloriosa lilies (red) and Variegated Sweet Flag.

196

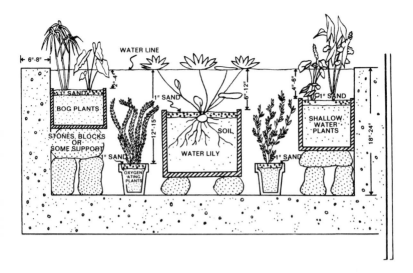

Proper planting methods.

YOUENS AFTER TRICKER

Fill Pool Before Planting

Prepare all the necessary containers, place them at the proper levels (see diagram) and fill the pool with water. It is a very simple matter to plant Water lilies and aquatic plants in the soil below the surface of the water. It is important, however, that the crown of the Water lily (the growing end) be above the surface.

Soil

The best soil for Water lilies and aquatic plants is a mixture of three parts of good top soil and one part of thoroughly rotted cow manure—a heavy clayey soil is very satisfactory. Muck from swamps, soil from woods, peat moss and sand should NOT be used in the soil.

Planting

Hardy Water lilies may be planted quite early in the spring but not until the water has warmed up so they will start immediately into new growth. In the latitude of Chicago, Cleveland and New

York, this date is usually toward the latter part of April. For tropical Water lilies the first week in June is usually the proper time in the same locality mentioned above. For points south of this line the date is, of course, earlier. Tropical Water lilies especially should be planted in full sunshine and in a depth of water from six to eight inches. Hardy Water lilies do best in a depth of water from eight to twelve inches. Plant lotuses in the same depth as the tropical Water lilies. While some do best in soil just covered with water, others do best in six inches of water. So, a happy medium can be met by using an average depth of three inches. (Consult diagram on page 197).

Lotus

Lotus tubers look very much like bananas. The usual cause of failure with Lotus is careless handling of the tubers, deep planting in soil, too great a depth of water or transplanting in cold water. They do need rich soil and plenty of room. Place the tuber in a horizontal position two inches below the surface of the soil and provide a depth of water four to six inches when first planted. After becoming well established, the depth of water can be increased to a maximum of twelve inches. But an average depth of eight inches of water is ideal. Handle tubers carefully in unpacking and planting so that the growing end is not broken. Pot plants are usually obtainable late in the season and are simply tubers started into growth in pots in tanks in greenhouses and when received are planted exactly the same as tropical Water lilies by pressing the ball of earth into the soft mud to a position just below the surface of the soil. All soil in pools should be covered with approximately one inch of clean sand which prevents any particles from the soil floating into the water and discoloring it.

Winter Care

The hardy varieties of Water lilies can be easily wintered if they are not allowed to freeze. The tender sorts, tropical Water lilies, had best be renewed each year if the best flowering results are to be expected, unless a greenhouse pool is available to which to move them. The one condition necessary for safe wintering of hardy Water lilies is to see that the roots are not actually frozen. Under natural conditions, hardy Water lilies, Lotus and native aquatics winter in the ponds under water and seldom need protection unless the water gets very low or the winter is most severe. In small pools where the hardy plants are planted in boxes or in the bottom of the pool, it is advisable to drain the pool and fill it with leaves. For larger pools where one intends to leave fish in the pool, it is advisable to cover the pool with shutters made of tightly fitting boards. On top of the boards may be raked a pile of leaves 12 to 15 inches thick. The leaves should extend beyond the edges of the pool. It is advisable to cover the leaves with corn stalks, brush or chicken wire to keep the leaves from blowing away. If the roots are planted in boxes, another method is to remove the boxes containing the roots and store in a cool basement, keeping them covered with moist peat moss, leaves or burlap until spring. This method is preferred to covering over the pool, a procedure which is not normally advised.

Pests

Many people fear that a pool may become a breeding place for mosquitos. This could easily happen, but is most successfully controlled by the introduction of goldfish into the pool. Goldfish will destroy mosquito wrigglers even before they become visible to the naked eye. The Black Aphis is the usual plant pest. It is easily controlled by a force of clean water or, in the cases of infestation, by spraying with an aquaticide sold specifically for pools.

Algae

Excessive algal growth can make the pool water dark green or slimy. Increasing the shade will usually correct this; or commercially available chemicals may be used to clear pools.

If the fish can be removed, add one ounce (by weight) of copper sulphate (see Chapter IX—Diseases) to each 8,000 gallons (US) of water in the pool. Drain, flush and refill the pool after treatment. If it is not possible to remove the fish, use $\frac{1}{8}$ ounce for each 2,500 gallons (US) of water. No water change is necessary after the milder treatment.

The broad-tailed types of nacreous Veiltails favored by British aquarists.

XIV   Goldfishkeeping in Great Britain

Goldfishkeeping in the British Isles appears a paradox in some respects. There are literally millions of goldfishes and carps living contented lives in garden ponds all over the country. In suburbia it is very fashionable to offset the lawn with a goldfish pool with, as like as not, a fountain gently spraying the surface. The Britisher loves his garden, but the six-foot hedge around the garden indicates his insularity. By a process of trial and error, he discovers what is best for his fish and with that he is satisfied. Since the climate is semi-rigorous, the choice of outdoor varieties is automatically limited to the Common Goldfish and the Shubunkin, with the odd Fantail thrown in for those who want the unusual. In this sense the goldfish is the most popular of pets. The demand for this market is met by importations from Italy chiefly, and reasonably good specimens can be bought for less than 50 New Pence ($1.10

US) from the five hundred or so pet shops in the United Kingdom, one or more of which may be found in most towns.

Societies

For the enthusiast, there are nearly four hundred aquarium societies with an average membership of 25 to 30, each with its tropical and cold-water sections. Usually the goldfish sections are not so well supported as the tropical, and the Goldfish Society of Great Britain (GSGB) was formed 20 years ago to cater to these. Most aquarium societies are affiliated with the Federation of British Aquarium Societies. Except for the towns of Bristol and Birmingham, who are negotiating an agreement with the GSGB, most societies accept the standards of the GSGB and the Federation of British Aquarium Societies has officially adopted them. For all practical purposes, the GSGB is acknowledged as the organization in Britain best equipped to look after the interests of the goldfish.

Exhibitions

Three national exhibitions are held annually in Britain, one in the north and two in London, at each of which an attendance of 20,000 can be expected. Overall, one can say the Common, the Veiltail, the Moor, the Shubunkin, the Lionhead, the Oranda and the Fantail are the most popular varieties. It is left to the Annual Convention of the GSGB to put up additional classes for the Pom-pom [British spelling], the Pearl Scale, the Bubble-eye and the Celestial, which appeal more to the specialist. This annual convention is the only place in Britain where all the known mutations of the goldfish can be seen at one time under one roof, and demonstrates clearly the effort of the Society to protect and perpetuate the work of centuries. Every encouragement is given to members to breed the popular and not-so-popular varieties, and the standards have been laid down to this end. For example, all the mutants have been incorporated into eight basic varieties and provision made in the pointing to cover the three scale groups for each. Thus, the Metallic Veiltail can be shown in one class with the matt and the nacreous, with justice to all three scale groups. The broad forkless caudal fin is the prerogative of the Veiltail, and this mutation is found in no other variety recognized by the

A male Shubunkin showing tubercles on the gill covers and pectoral fins. In England, a Shubunkin with this type of tail is called a "Bristol" Shubunkin.

GSGB. As the Society holds that each mutation should be developed to its logical limit, the partial development of the head hood is not recognized and the hood of the Lionhead must completely envelop the head. These are just examples of the specialist approach by British breeders to their subject, and if results are anything to go by, the end justifies the means.

By outlawing crossbreeding, the majority of breeders have established strains which are breeding true to type, so mongrel fishes, especially the throwbacks, are seldom (if ever) seen on the showbench.

Commercially Speaking

In Great Britain most goldfish breeding is done by amateurs.

Several attempts have been made by the trade to set up fish farms and breeding establishments, but these, with one or two exceptions, have failed. They find that it is more profitable to buy one-inch fry from abroad and grow them to size. Land is expensive, heating costs are high and clean natural water more and more difficult to discover. Water lily nurserymen combine fish and plants happily, but the frequency of cold summers requires the purchase of stock that has already turned color. The poor return for live trout has tempted several trout farmers to go over to goldfish, but here again without marked success. Speaking broadly, the professional goldfish breeder does not exist in Britain, and except for the fish imported, amateurs and semi-professionals (those using breeding as a sideline) supply the market for those varieties which need more than open earth ponds for propagation.

The goldfish is a man-made fish and the fascination of the study lies in the steady upgrading of the percentage breeding true to type. Not until strains breed 90 per cent true to type can we afford to relax and, in my opinion, not until then will the goldfish come into its own rightful place in the hobby. The aim of the GSGB is to produce strains of fish with a high quality potential which are vigorous and hardy, and this is being done by paying attention to correct line breeding, as in other comparable fields. There are signs that aquarists in Britain are ready for this, and new recruits are coming in constantly.

International Standards

Perhaps the time is ripe for international cooperation. Now that the mutations for Bubble-eye, Pom-pom, Celestial and Pearl Scale have become available in larger numbers, a move could be made to consolidate the available knowledge gained in the various countries. This could take the form in the initial stages of a meeting of the leading authorities from each interested country to draw up a format of proposals, which could then go back to each country for discussion. Once everyone knows how the others feel, the prospect for universal agreement should not be far away, and a convention can be organized for the final agreement. Since the United States lies at a geographically convenient point between East and West, perhaps they would act as hosts.

Japanese Ribbontail or Ryūkin. This is the type which has done so much to popularize the goldfish in Japan.

XV A Summary

What has been written will, I hope, be helpful to you in spawning, hatching, raising and enjoying your fish. In closing, I would like to emphasize the following points:

Size of Container

Whether goldfish are raised in tanks or in ponds, the more space they can be given, the more successful your efforts will be. You may have temporary success in crowding a lot of fish into a small tank, but these fish are less able to withstand any stress or calamity —whether it be a period of time where the oxygen is low or when some disease gains a foothold. Give your fish plenty of room.

Feeding

Goldfish which are put on the market have been subjected to a period of starvation, since this makes the fish easier to ship and enables them to withstand the crowded conditions which the dealer must maintain. When these fish are first brought home, they should be fed very sparingly since their digestive systems have become somewhat atrophied; feed them only small amounts at a time, gradually increasing the amount daily.

Any reference work on goldfish, and even the directions on fish food packages, warn against overfeeding fish. Fish rarely overeat, but an excess of uneaten food will foul the water and kill the fish, while too rich a diet may eventually cause internal disorders.

Sunlight

It is hard to realize just how important sunlight is for goldfish. It is true that they are water creatures, but even so, some sun is indispensable for their good health.

Temperature

Goldfish are poikilothermic, which means that they have no internal temperature-regulating mechanism and must assume the temperature of their surrounding water. In spite of this, they are able to withstand great variations in temperature. These variations can be tolerated as long as the changes are gradual. When goldfish are moved from one place to another, we must make sure that they are not subjected to a *sudden* change of temperature, or they may die or be so weakened that disease can gain a foothold.

Green Water

Within limits, green water is the best environment in which to keep goldfish. But, while green water is good for goldfish, the amount of algae causing the color must be controlled so that the water maintains a certain clarity. A good rule of thumb is to be certain that you can see the fish through ten or twelve inches of the green water. When the water becomes greener than this, with a high density of algae, it is time to reduce the light. Aquarium algaecides are available, and using them at half-strength will usually weaken the algae without destroying them all.

Simplification

Do not attempt to keep too many goldfish. A few well-chosen fish will give much pleasure, but if an attempt is made to keep too many, the work involved will soon outweigh the pleasure. If we are hoping to breed our goldfish, it is probably best to keep only one variety and to concentrate our efforts on breeding the best of this type.

Koi, like goldfish, are naturally tame and respond readily to regular feeding. They will even submit to being petted. This type is called Hariwake Ōgon.

XVI Carp

Nishiki Goi (The Brocaded Carp, or Colored Carp)

Colored Carp symbolize Japan even more than goldfish do. "The Fifth of May" is "Children's Day," a major Japanese holiday, and on this day families display colorful cloth carp on flagpoles to announce the recent birth of a male infant.

All Colored Carp are variations on the Common Carp (*Cyprinus carpio*), differing from the Wild Carp and from each other only in color. While the Common Carp is found in a wild state in many parts of the world, only in recent years have many specimens of the Colored Carp been seen outside of Japan. The ready availability of air transport now makes it possible to send good specimens all over the world.

Since goldfish are familiar to almost everyone, a good introduction to the Colored Carp would be a brief description of the ways in which they differ from the goldfish. Although technically goldfish are carp also, we use the word carp here to refer to the Brocaded Carp, Nishiki Goi, as well as to the wild form, Ma Goi. The word "Goi" alone or, as it is commonly spelled, "Koi," means carp. "Nishiki" means brocaded.

Both goldfish and carp belong to the same family, *Cyprinidae*. Goldfish are bred from Crucian Carp (Silver Carp), with which they are genetically identical; therefore, they should have the same scientific name, *Carassius carassius*. Traditionally, however, goldfish are named *Carassius auratus* and Crucian Carp remains *Carrassius carassius*. The Koi is descended from the Wild Carp (*Cyprinus carpio*), an entirely different genus.

Colored Carp grow much larger than do goldfish. But goldfish liberated in lakes and ponds will grow quite large (though not as large as large carp), and eventually will revert to the ancestral wild type. They may reach a length of 12 to 14 inches and are often erroneously called "Red Carp." Among these fish there are often some specimens which retain the bright colors of the cultivated goldfish.

The one obvious difference between goldfish and carp is that carp have little moustaches, two pairs of "barbels." There are other less obvious differences which the scientist might note, such as the dorsal fin. In carp the dorsal fin has three hard rays succeeded by 17 to 20 soft rays, whereas the goldfish has three hard rays succeeded by 14 to 18 soft rays. Once one has seen a few specimens of carp and has compared them to goldfish it becomes a simple matter to distinguish between the two.

Occasionally specimens of carp are artificially crossed with goldfish. The males of these hybrids are infertile, but it is probable that the females are not. Unlike the goldfish there are still no varieties of carp with fins differing radically from those of the wild type fish.

All of the carp breeders' efforts have been concentrated on developing the coloration, and today carp are truly the most colorful of all the aquarium fishes. The best specimens actually have colors which are more striking and vivid than the brilliant hues of saltwater fishes found near coral reefs. With such brilliant coloration it is just as well that carp were never developed for variations in body shape and fins, since this would only distract from one's appreciation of the incomparable coloring.

The History of Ornamental Carp

It is generally agreed that the Wild Carp (Ma Goi) (*Cyprinus carpio*), had its origin in Central Asia. These carp were esteemed as food fish and it was natural that men would bring carp with them as they migrated from place to place, for use as a medium of barter. Hardy fish, carp soon established themselves in the waters wherever they were introduced. Because of their ability to survive under less than favorable conditions, carp have been accused of displacing more desirable sport fishes. This is not really true. Carp have their own ecological niche, which is another way of saying that they thrive only when conditions are right for them, and they are not likely to displace fish, such as trout or bass, which do best in an environment which is not suitable for carp. Waters in which trout would thrive would not encourage carp and the reverse is true. However, under some circumstances carp may change the characteristics of a particular body of water because of their habit of eating vegetation and churning up the bottom in their search for food. The introduction of carp, or for that matter of any other fish, to any public water is something that should be left to the biologist and wildlife specialist.

The introduction of carp to Japan dates back hundreds of years. In the Nihonshoki, or old chronicles of Japan, it is written that Emperor Keiko watched carp being released into a pond in AD 94.

A pair of Mirror Carp (*Cyprinus carpio*). These are a domesticated variety of the Common Carp. Through breeding, the scales have been almost totally eliminated. Those remaining are in a straight line paralleling the lateral line. In poor specimens the scales are scattered at random.

BARRY PENGILLEY

The Nihonshoki does not say whether these were colored carp. In AD 265–316 there are writings from China which refer to colored carp. These Chinese writings mention red, blue, black, white and yellow carp.

Gray, wild Colored Carp were raised as food fish, but even these carp found a place in the affections of the Japanese and Chinese, and they were believed to be good omens. Though they were destined to be eaten, they were still thought of as pets. It was therefore natural that a color mutation of the carp would not pass unnoticed, and that when a colored carp was found it would receive special care and attempts would be made to breed it. Undoubtedly, this is how the first strains of Colored Carp were established. It is likely that these early fish were of a single color, either red or yellow.

The Japanese garden, whether large or small, usually has a pond in it, and the Colored Carp were soon being kept for their ornamental value rather than as a prospective meal. Like goldfish, the Colored Carp were at first cultivated only by the nobility and the wealthy who had their beautiful gardens in Kyoto, the ancient capital of Japan. Afer a period of time, the common people took up something which had first been reserved for the upper classes.

After the Meiji Restoration in 1868, farmers began keeping carp for their enjoyment and recreation during the winter months when they had no work in the fields to occupy their time. In the Niigata Prefecture, the farmers would build a pond, one part of which would extend inside the house, and during the winter the Colored Carp would swim into the house out of the cold, and be fed by the farmer's family. In this way, the big carp soon became household pets.

During the warmer times of the year, the farmers held competitive exhibitions at which their beloved Colored Carp were shown. This competition sharpened the efforts to breed more colorful fish; the strains of carp improved year by year and carp breeding became, for the Niigata farmers, a principal form of recreation.

In 1914, the third year of Taishō, the beautiful carp from Niigata attracted large crowds at Tokyo's Ueno Park, where they were shown at the Grand Exhibition. The striking beauty of these carp was greatly admired, and it was at this time that they

Aka Muji. This is a remarkable example of deep scarlet coloration.

were given the name Nishiki Goi, Brocaded Carp.

The demand for the Nishiki Goi increased so greatly after the Grand Exhibition that professional breeders began raising them. Today these breeders are constantly attempting to produce improved and more beautiful strains of fish.

Other areas of Japan now share in the production of Nishiki Goi. Kōriyama in Nara, Hiroshima and Yamaguchi are centers for Nishiki Goi culture. Still, Niigata continues to lead in producing Nishiki Goi, and the best carp come from there. Over ten million Nishiki Goi come out of the Niigata Prefecture ponds each year, and these bring in more than eight hundred thousand dollars a year to the breeders.

Carp fanciers gather in large numbers at the competitions, where the best Nishiki Goi vie with each other for the top prizes. The best known of these shows is held at Ojiya in Niigata, and this show attracts carp-lovers from as far away as Kyūshū and Shikoku.

Today the popularity of Nishiki Goi is at an all-time high. The success of the breeders in producing good strains, the discovery of successful methods of maintaining carp in small ponds, and the facilities for successfully transporting these large fish promise to keep Nishiki Goi in fashion for many years to come.

Outside of Japan, Nishiki Goi are being introduced to more and more people because of the fast air transportation from Japan to all parts of the world, and in years to come these carp will be valued pets in many countries.

Varieties of the Japanese Colored Carp

All of the varieties of the carp we will discuss here belong to the same species, *Cyprinus carpio*, and even though there is only one recognized scientific name for all of these fish, different Japanese names are given to the various well-known color patterns. For the most part these colors and patterns do not breed true; still, it will add to our enjoyment of these carp if we know the Japanese names and their meanings, and understand how these names were derived.

The Colored Carp are roughly divided into two groups. The first are the monotone carps, that is, those having only one color; the second are the patterned carps with two or more colors. The patterns of carp differ from each other in the same way that the faces of human beings do, and there is about the same chance of finding two carp with exactly the same pattern. As we said, the patterned carp do not breed true, so it is easy to see that in order to produce a good specimen it is necessary to cull and select from thousands of fry.

A living kaleidoscope. This picture was not taken in Japan, but in a fancier's establishment in Ohio. DONALD DADY AND EUGENE KRYGOWSKI

When writing for Western readers, Japanese writers use Roman letters for transliterating (spelling out pronunciation); this system is termed Rōmaji in Japanese. In addition to the traditional Rōmaji spellings, we will supply modified phonetic symbols where necessary.

In most cases, Japanese is evenly pronounced, with no special emphasis on a syllable—or at least no emphasis as in English, although the Japanese do have some ways of differently emphasizing words of the same spelling with different meanings. However, it is usually quite difficult for foreigners to imitate Japanese pronunciation, and since it is not the purpose of this book to teach Japanese we shall give only a few simple rules and indications.

Every letter should be pronounced, and pronounced only in one way, roughly equivalent to the Latin value. With the qualifications below, the approximate English values hold true.

Every syllable is pronounced separately: [sanke] is "sahn kay," not "sang-kay." Every sound is pronounced: [sake] is "sah kay" rather than as in the English "for goodness sake." Do not make diphthongs (double vowels): [muji] is "moo jee," not "myoo jee" like the English "*music.*"

Usually a syllable is composed of one consonant and one vowel—exceptions are such combinations as "tsu" and "nya," and of course transcriptional customs like "shi" and "chi."

Phonetic symbols are always enclosed in brackets, [], and punctuation, capitalization, etc., are not included.

[a]	=	*a*ha	[e]	=	b*e*t	[i]	=	b*i*t
[a:]	=	f*a*ther	[e:]	=	(approximately*) fete	[i:]	=	b*ie*r

	[o]	=	h*o*rn	[u]	=	r*u*le	
	[o:]	=	(approximately*) sh*o*w				

[ai]	=	h*i*de	[oi]	=	J*oey*	[ui]	=	g*ooey*

[ch]	=	*ch*air	[g]	=	*g*o	[j]	=	*j*udge
[sh]	=	*sh*eep	[ts]	=	fa*ts*o	[ny]	=	o*ni*on

*The pure vowels [e:] and [o:] do not exist in English, our closest equivalents occurring in diphthongs. [e:] is found at the beginning of the "ay" in "bay"—if you stop short before reaching the "y," the sound will closely resemble [e:]. [o:] is most closely approximated, similarly, by stopping before the "w" in "show;" here, however, the sound should be slightly colored towards the vowel in the word "ball."

212

Note that a colon after a vowel has the effect of lengthening it. Do not give the vowel a long pronunciation unless it is so marked.

Commonly Used Carp Terms

Koi	Carp. If it has a modifying word before it, it is often changed into Goi, as in Hi Goi, Doitsu Goi.
Ma Goi	Wild Carp. Rarely kept in ponds today except when cultivated as a food fish.
Moyō Goi	Patterned Carp. Carp adorned with some color other than the main color. It is impossible to have two carp with exactly the same pattern. Kōhaku, Utsuri Goi, Bekko belong to this classification.
Nishiki Goi	Name given to good specimens of Hi Goi. Nishiki means brocaded.
Akame	Red-eyed, as seen in Ki Goi and Shiro Muji. Indicates that these are albino or semi-albino fish, having no melanophores.
Doitsu	German. Used to indicate the two carp types which are considered of German origin: the Mirror Carp and Leather Carp. Mirror Carp have few, irregularly spaced large scales. Leather Carp have no scales.

A Japanese classification of Hi Goi body types. The vast majority are types "C" and "D" or fall somewhere in between.   DONALD DADY AND EUGENE KRYGOWSKI

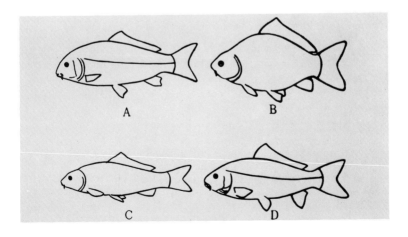

	Doitsu is used as a prefix, as in Doitsu Sanshoku, Doitsu Asagi, Doitsu Ōgon, Doitsu Kōhaku, etc.
Gin	Silver. Used as Gin Rin, or silver scales; Gin Kabuto, or Silver Helmet.
Hi Goi	Hi means red, and Hi Goi would translate as red carp; but the term Hi Goi is used most often to refer to all colored carp in order to differentiate them from the wild carp of Ma Goi.
Iro Koi	Colored Carp. Used like Hi Goi, to mean any colored carp.
Kabuto	The helmet worn by the ancient Japanese samurai. Used when a contrasting color on the head is thought to resemble the samurai helmet.

Kōhaku [ko: haku]

Kō means red, haku means white; so the Kōhaku is a white carp with a red pattern. This is one of the most popular of the colored carp.

An outstanding specimen of Kōhaku is almost sure to be a prize-winner at a competitive show. While Kōhaku can be bought at low prices, a topnotch Kōhaku is still considered a prize fish. The best Kōhaku must show a pure red and not just a variant color in a particular area or from place to place. The pattern of red over the white body is also critical in the selection of a first-class fish. Extensive deep red patterns are superior to small, light red patterns. Since the carp is usually viewed from above, the big, deep-red pattern should be borne along the dorsal part, starting at the head and going all the way back to the caudal area. Symmetry seen in the patterning as viewed from above is greatly desired.

If a Kōhaku has red lips, it is called Kōhaku Kuchibeni (rouged Kōhaku). If the Kōhaku has Gin Rin (silvery, glittering scales) it is called Kōhaku Gin Rin.

Tanchō [tancho:]

Tanchō is a shortened form of Tanchō Zuru, the name of a crane (*Grus japonensis*) which has a white body with a red pattern on the head. In popular Japanese lore it is believed that this bird is

DONALD DADY AND EUGENE KRYGOWSKI

Kōhaku. While this is probably the most common variety, it is not at all easy to breed or buy one with brilliant, clear, silvery white and deep scarlet markings such as this. In 1965, in Honolulu, a ten inch female of this type sold for $2,000.

always happy and lives for a thousand years. The Tanchō is a sub-variety of Kōhaku, the red coloring showing up only on the head with the remainder of the body white. Tanchō are obtained by strict selection from Kōhaku fry. It is very rare to come across the ideal type of Tanchō, which has a round, red marking on top, right in the center of the head. The Tanchō is at its best when it is

3 years old or older, since at that age the whiteness of the fish becomes greatly intensified. All Colored Carp are at their best as they grow older.

Shiro Muji

Shiro means white, Muji means nothing else; so Shiro Muji means all white.

When the fish is fully grown, its pristine white is very striking, but on an all-white carp marrings caused by parasites and scars or blemishes are very noticeable. Because of this, it must be handled with special care. When roughly handled or transported for long distances, the fish may pick up a temporary reddish tinge, due to irritation and expansion of the capillaries (small blood vessels) in the skin.

Albino Shiro Muji with red eyes do exist, but most Shiro Muji are not albino and have normal black eyes. Shiro Muji are usually bred from Kōhaku.

Aka Muji

Aka means red, so Aka Muji is an all-red fish. The red becomes more intense as the fish grows, and the deeper the red, the better the fish. The redness in the Aka Muji is due to a high accumulation of erythrophores, which are orange pigment cells, and to xanthophores, which are yellow pigment cells, both of which in combination and in sufficient number can produce a true, deep red color.

This carp must be exposed to sunlight, or its red color will fade to a yellowish-orange

The color of this carp is also affected by its diet, and feeding it dried shrimp, egg yolk or live foods such as earthworms, *Tubifex*, or *Chironomus* larvae helps to intensify the color. Some authorities claim that the quality of the water has a great deal to do with the color, but there is no general agreement on the best way to produce the desired red color. It is assumed that the genetic makeup of the carp is at least as important in determining its redness as the other factors. Even in the best specimens, the redness of the Aka Muji never quite reaches the intensity of the red color seen in patches on the best specimens of Kōhaku or Sanshoku. The reason for this is probably that the pigments which make up the red color are much more concentrated when they appear in patches than when spread over the entire body of the fish. A full-grown Aka Muji is a very splendid fish to behold, with its rows of glittering scales. When the refractive scales appear on the red it is called Kin Rin; when they appear on the white it is called Gin Rin. Aka Muji is another fish whose parents are almost always Kōhaku.

Shiro Bekko

Bekko means turtle shell. When a white carp has black dots on it, it is called Shiro Bekko.

The major part of this carp must be pure white, and the black dots must be clear and velvet black. This is another variety that has to grow to a sufficient size in order to be fully appreciated. Coloring on this carp is not as vivid as on some of the other types, but it seems to be admired for its plain and understated beauty.

Aka Bekko

A red carp with black dots is called Aka Bekko. The main part of the body must be pure red, and the black dots again must be clear, velvet black. It is considered ideal if the black dots are scattered only along the dorsal part of the body and the lower part is clear.

Taishō Sanshoku or Taishō Sanke

Taishō in the name of this carp refers to the era of Emperor Taishō (1912–1926), during whose reign the fish was produced. Sanshoku, or Sanke, means three-colored. The basic color of this carp is white, with red and black patterns well proportioned in the dorsal area. The red and black areas should be distinct from each other and not overlap. These patterns are sought in the dorsal area, and as much symmetry as possible is desired.

The Taishō Sanshoku with Gin Rin (silvery, glittering scales) or Kuchibeni (red lips) is also a highly admired type. Top specimens of Taishō Sanshoku often command a price of more than five thousand dollars.

Taishō Sanshoku. This beautiful fish was named in honor of Emperor Taishō.

Ki Goi

Ki means yellow, Goi means carp. Therefore, Ki Goi means yellow carp. There are two kinds of Ki Goi. One has no melanin (black pigment) and is red-eyed, the other has normal black eyes. The red-eyed Ki Goi are considered to be a type of albino or semi-albino.

The scales of these carp are rich in xanthophores, the yellow pigment cells. Since this carp is an all-yellow monotone and we have now learned a few words of Japanese, we might think it ought to be called "Ki Muji," but the usual name for this fish in Japan is Ki Goi. In an ideal specimen the yellow would extend into the underparts. The fins too should be yellow.

If a red-eyed carp is crossed with some other carp with black eyes, all of the fry will have black eyes.

Shōwa Sanshoku or **Shōwa Sanke** [sho:wa sanshoku, sho:wa sanke]

Shōwa in the name of this carp refers to the era of the Emperor Shōwa (1926–present), during whose reign the fish was developed. This is a tri-colored carp like the Taishō Sanshoku, but on the Shōwa Sanshoku, black is the background color on which patterns of red and white are scattered. It is a darker fish than the

Taishō Sanshoku. No one could fail to be impressed by this gorgeous red, black and white carp. The evenness, intensity and distribution of color are particularly good.

DONALD DADY AND EUGENE KRYGOWSKI

Taishō Sanshoku, with some specimens having a bluish sheen on the back as one of their most striking characteristics.

In Japan, when we say Sanshoku, we are usually referring to Taishō Sanshoku. Shōwa Sanshoku and Taishō Sanshoku have different ancestries, even though their names may sound similar. The Shōwa Sanshoku may sometimes be thought of as the Shiro Utsuri with the addition of red dots.

Utsuri Mono

Utsuri means changing color, and Mono means thing or carp. The basic color of the fish in this group is black, over which patterns of other colors are scattered.

Shiro Utsuri

The color pattern on this carp is just the reverse of Shiro Bekko—white on a black background. On Shiro Utsuri the white is often not a pure white.

It may well be said that Shiro Utsuri is the Shōwa Sanshoku with the red patterns missing. The black areas on these fish should be as dark as possible.

Hi Utsuri

Hi Utsuri is a black carp adorned with scarlet or reddish patterns. Though this fish has the same colors as Aka Bekko, the background and pattern have been reversed. Hi Utsuri is a carp of rather ancient lineage.

Ki Utsuri

Ki Utsuri is a black carp adorned with a yellow pattern. It is seen less frequently than Hi Utsuri, and it may be said that the Ki Utsuri is a Hi Utsuri with lighter colors.

Kin Utsuri

Kin means gold, and this is a black carp with touches of glittering gold scales scattered over the body. One of the parents for this fish might be a type of Hikari Mono. A counterpart—that is, a gold carp with black dots—has recently appeared. It is called Tora Ōgon, although it should more properly be called Kin Bekko.

Cha Goi

Cha means brown or chocolate brown. This is another of the monotone or single-colored carp. It was produced by crossing an albino white (Akame Shiro Muji) and Ma Goi (wild-type carp). The color on this carp varies somewhat according to the environment of the pond. It is not a very popular carp, being rather sober in coloration.

Asagi

Asagi means blue or light blue. This carp has a blue or light blue back and a reticulated scale pattern. This is a very old strain of Colored Carp, and many others, such as the Shūsui, have been produced from it; but the Asagi is not as colorful as the Shūsui.

Matsuba

The literal translation of Matsuba is "the leaf of the pine tree." The color on the scales is reticulated as it is in Asagi. This carp has brownish colors which recall the withered needles of pine trees. This is also a rather soberly colored carp.

Shūsui [shu:sui]

This carp was produced by Kichigorō Akiyama, Sr., a famous Japanese breeder in the Meiji (1868–1912) and Taishō (1912–1926) eras, by crossing German Mirror Carp and the Japanese Asagi. It has mirror-type scales; the upper part of the body is sky blue, the blue becoming lighter down the sides, and the ventral side as red as the morning glow. As mentioned above, this is a carp of rather old origin, and it is a pity that a typical Shūsui can rarely be seen lately. These days, any Mirror Carp with red and blue is called Shūsui, even though the color arrangement may be very different from that of the true Shūsui carp.

Hikari Mono

Carp of this group have glittering metallic scales scattered over their bodies. They are also called Ōgon, which means golden. If the word Ōgon is part of the name of a carp, it is one of the Hikari Mono group.

The Ōgon was produced by Sawata Awoki and his son, and it has since been used to improve the other strains of Colored Carp.

There are many color varieties in the Hikari Mono group; the thing that distinguishes them is the distinctive glittering metallic scalation.

Ōgon [o:gon]

Ōgon is the golden fish with the glittering scales all over the body. This was the first of the fish produced in Niigata Prefecture by Sawata Awoki and his son, after 30 years of strenuous efforts. Ōgon has a tendency to turn blackish in color when the water temperature is high, or if the environment otherwise does not suit it. This tendency to turn dark depends to a large extent on the genetic quality of the strain—a good strain of Ōgon is not likely to lose its glittering gold tint in any environment. When we see these Ōgons swimming in the sun, we are at a loss for words with which to describe their striking beauty.

Orenji Ōgon [orenji o:gon]

This is an orange-colored Ōgon and was produced soon after the original golden Ōgon. This orange color is produced by a combination of erythrophores, xanthophores and guanophores.

Kin Kabuto

The Kin Kabuto, or Golden Helmet, is a carp which is gold only on the head, the remainder of the body void of glittering gold scales. It was replaced by a good specimen of the Ōgon.

Yamabuki Ōgon [yamabuki o:gon]

Yamabuki is the name of a Japanese plant (*Kerria japonica*) which has yellow flowers. This carp might well be described as a Ki Goi with glittering scales. The yellow in this fish is due to an abundance of xanthophore in the scales.

Nezu Ōgon [nezu o:gon]

Nezu is the abridged form of nezumi iro, which means grayish color. The glitter here is more subdued than in either the Ōgon or the Yamabuki Ōgon.

Kujyaku Ōgon [kujyaku o:gon]

Kujyaku means peacock. This fish has varied colors and glittering scales, and it is considered somewhat gaudy.

Hariwake Ōgon [hariwake o:gon]

The body of this carp is divided into two types of Ōgon; some parts are Nezu Ōgon, and others ordinary Ōgon. One of its faults is that the Nezu portions at times gradually fade away and become ordinary Ōgon. The reason for this color change is not known.

Purachina Ōgon [purachina o:gon]

Purachina means platinum; this is a platinum-colored fish.

Koi are not territorial creatures. They live peacefully together even when there is a considerable difference in size.

XVII   The Care of Carp

Generally speaking, if one follows the same technique as for keeping goldfish outdoors, the basic needs of the carp will be met. Since carp grow larger than goldfish, more space must be allotted for the individual carp than for the goldfish. Carp are at their best when they are permitted to reach their normal size, so we should give them adequate growing room. Carp are mild fish and will not fight each other, nor will they harm smaller fish in the pond. They are hardy fish, do not require heat in the winter except in the colder areas and are not particularly prone to disease.

If we should acquire a few small carp, we might want to keep them in a glass tank, where all of their beautiful colors can be seen to full advantage. It is unfortunate that the color of carp kept indoors is generally not as vivid as those of their brothers in the garden pool. In the tank, the carp can be a rather quiet creature and may not show all of the activity we come to expect from other aquarium fishes. Outdoors, in a well-managed pool, carp will be active and we can enjoy watching them as they mature and reach their full potential in size and beauty.

Whether in a tank or in a pool, the carp does not require crystal-clear water; but if we are to admire and display our prize specimens, it is necessary that some thought be given to keeping the water reasonably clear. This can be managed through adroit water changing, shading the water to keep it from becoming too green from the sun or employment of a filtration system. One way to keep the water clear and to generally avoid trouble is not to overcrowd the carp pond. An approximate guide to the number of carp which may be kept in a pond without aeration is as follows:

Area of the pond in square feet	Depth of the pond in inches	Size of the carp in inches	Number of carp
16	12	6–8	1– 15
50– 65	12–20	6–8	30– 40
130–165	16–24	12	10– 15
650	24	12	60–100
		18	40– 50
		24	20– 30

If the pond is aerated or filtered, the number of fish may be doubled or tripled. As there are so many variables, a table of this type cannot be relied upon completely, and our own observations will best tell us if the carp are healthy. If the carp are found gasping at the top of the water for air, even occasionally, we know that the pond is either already overcrowded or on the verge. This may also happen if the water is too warm, because as the water warms, progressively less oxygen will be available. Therefore, it is better that the pond be somewhat underpopulated, since when a pond is filled to its capacity with carp, the growth and development of the fish will be retarded. The depth of the pond is not too important, except that in the colder areas it should be deep enough so that freezing will not harm the fish. If we plan to keep carp as large as two feet long, a water depth of at least two feet should be provided.

The cautions set forth in the goldfish section for good water hygiene should be followed in the carp pond; the carp is perhaps a bit more sensitive than is the goldfish, particularly with regard to oxygen content. The pH of water for carp should be around 7, and should never fall below 5 or rise above 9.

Gravel is not particularly recommended for the bottom of the carp pond, since they will be constantly rooting in it, and a gravel-free pond is less trouble to maintain.

Carp are to a great extent vegetarians, and plants such as *Vallisneria*, *Sagittaria*, *Cabomba* or Anacharis are likely to be eaten or uprooted when they are hungry; but plants like Water lilies and Spatterdock, which have their leaves above the water, and sturdy plants like Water hyacinth or Water lettuce will survive in the carp pond and add to its harmony and beauty. Some plants, particularly the Water lilies, do best when they are well fertilized, but we must be careful, since an excess of fertilizer can spoil the water and kill off the carp.

Food

While carp are basically vegetarians, they will eat almost all the things that we think of as suitable for fish food. They particularly like live foods such as earthworms, bloodworms (*Chironomus* larvae), mosquito wrigglers, *Tubifex*, or *Daphnia*, and these live foods are particularly good for the young carp.

As the carp grow larger they consume so much food that it can soon become too much trouble or too much of an expense to feed them sufficient quantities of live food, so that we have to turn to some type of dry or prepared food. In feeding dry food, the same precautions must be observed as with goldfish, and the carp must not be overfed. With the larger quantities of food which carp consume, we might find it advantageous to make up some of the goldfish formula, or else purchase prepared food, in larger quantities, from suppliers of animal feeds. Equal amounts of rabbit pellets, which are largely vegetable matter, and trout pellets, which contain more animal matter, would be a good basic diet for carp. Whole wheat bread is also a good supplement to the carp diet, and this has the advantage of floating so that we may observe the carp feeding.

The caution on feeding is, again, do not overfeed and never give the carp more food than they can eat in ten minutes at one time. If any food is uneaten after ten minutes it should be removed.

Light

Fish like goldfish and carp are most colorful when they are looked at in a position which allows the light to reflect from them. It is advisable to locate our pond so that the carp can be seen with the sun glistening on their backs. It is believed that sunshine intensifies the red tints of the carp, although no one has ever given the scientific reasons why this should be so.

In the summer, if the sun is likely to heat the water over 88°F, some provision must be made for shade.

In some gardens, artificial lights are kept over the pond in order to display the fish to visitors; these lights have the added advantage of attracting the night insects which will fall into the water where they are relished by the fish. All of the insects do not fall into the water, however, and we might find we are drawing more insects than we want for our own comfort or for the health of our plantings around the pond.

Temperature

The carp grows best when the temperature is between 64° and 72°F, but can endure the cold waters beneath the winter ice. They feed best when the water temperature is above 56°F, but carp that have been kept all year round in water of about 48°F will become accustomed to feeding regularly at this lower temperature. However, they will not spawn, and they become fat.

In order to spawn carp, a temperature above 56°F is necessary, but aside from spawning we do not have to worry much about water temperature. Naturally, a sudden change in temperature can be harmful, and we should take the usual precautions to protect the fish against this.

Maintenance of the Pond

Carp live in rivers and ponds with mud bottoms, and they like to search in the mud for their food; so some mud in the bottom of our carp pond is not necessarily harmful to the fish. The mud can be rather useful in absorbing gases from decaying leaves and fish excrement, and can also work as a buffer in adjusting the pH of the pond water. However, when the mud has absorbed all of the gas it can hold, it is then likely to become a site for noxious bacteria and other harmful organisms and must be replaced.

Even if the water in the pond remains clear, a layer of mud and mulm will build up on the bottom and should be removed periodically. March or April is a good time to do this job, and again in the autumn after the leaves have stopped falling the pond should be given a final cleaning so that the fish may winter in safe surroundings.

A word of caution: when cleaning the pond, care must be taken to see that the carp are getting sufficient oxygen in whatever temporary container they are being kept in, and they must also be watched or covered, since carp can—and do—jump, especially if they are trying to escape from unfamiliar surroundings.

The waterfall serves a dual purpose, both aerating the water as it splashes and serving as a decorative focal point. Natural, biological filtering action takes ▶ place as the water splashes over the rocks—this tends to clarify as well as aerate the water.

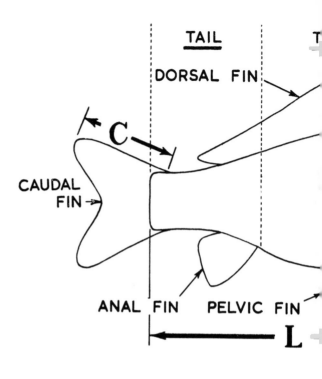

Appendix

The standards of The Goldfish Society of Great Britain are recognized throughout the world as authoritative. With the kind permission of the Club we are reproducing standards for only the six best known varieties.

The complete Standards may be obtained by writing to:

The Goldfish Society of Great Britain
Hon. Secretary: W. L. Wilson, Esq.
57, Constable Gardens
Edgeware, Middlesex, England

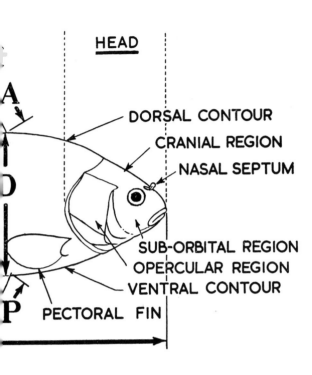

HEAD

DORSAL CONTOUR

CRANIAL REGION

NASAL SEPTUM

SUB-ORBITAL REGION

OPERCULAR REGION

VENTRAL CONTOUR

PECTORAL FIN

Legend for Drawing

A.   Anterior margin of dorsal fin.

C.   Dorsal lobe of caudal fin.

D.   Depth of body.

D/L. The ratio of depth of body to length of body.

L.   Length of body.

P.   Length of pelvic fin.

Characteristics: Intensity of color and carriage of caudal fin.

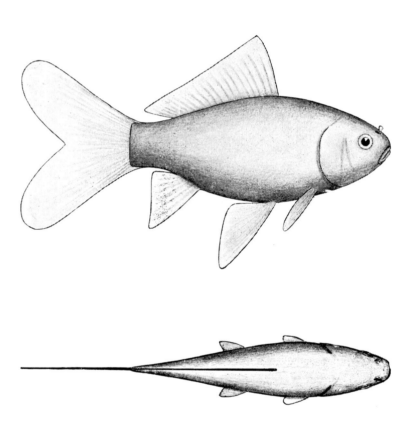

G.S.G.B. BRISTOL TYPE SHUBUNKIN
and GOLDFISH
(singletail)

Type Test

Fishes failing this test will be disqualified

1. Depth of body—between $\frac{3}{8}$ and $\frac{3}{7}$ length of body ($\frac{3}{8}$ to $\frac{3}{7}$ L).
2. Caudal fin—single and appearing well spread.
3. Length of dorsal lobe of caudal fin—greater than $\frac{3}{8}$ body length ($\frac{3}{8}$ L plus).
4. Extremities of fins—having rounded appearance.
5. Minimum length of body—$3\frac{1}{2}''$.

Standard Fishes

1. Depth of body—$\frac{2}{5}$ length of body ($\frac{2}{5}$ L).
2. Dorsal, lobe of caudal fin—$\frac{1}{2}$ body length ($\frac{1}{2}$ L).
3. Caudal fin—forked $\frac{1}{3}$.
4. Dorsal margin of caudal fin—approximating to a straight line.
5. Length of anterior margin of dorsal fin—$\frac{1}{4}$ body length ($\frac{1}{4}$ L).
6. Length of pelvic fins—$\frac{1}{3}$ body length ($\frac{1}{3}$ L).

Points Table

Body					Fins	
D/L ratio	...	...	...	8	Contour and size of Dorsal ...	6
Dorsal contour (including					Contour and size of Caudal ...	8
nasal septum)	...	...	5		Contour and size of others ...	5
Ventral contour	...	...	5			—
Lateral contour	...	...	3			19
Eyes and mouth	...	...	3			—
				—		
				24		
				—		

Colour

Bristol Goldfish Metallic Group					Bristol Shubunkin Other Groups (Calico)		
Orange	...	...	...	14	Blue		9
Silver ...	...	...	...	5	Orange or Yellow		5
				—	Black		5
				19			19
				—			—
Self-Orange	...	...	...	19			
				—			

Condition and Deportment					Special Characteristic		
Condition	...	...	...	10	Intensity of colour		7
Deportment	...	...	...	9	Carriage of caudal fin ...		12
				19			19
				—			—

Characteristics: Development of caudal and dorsal fins.

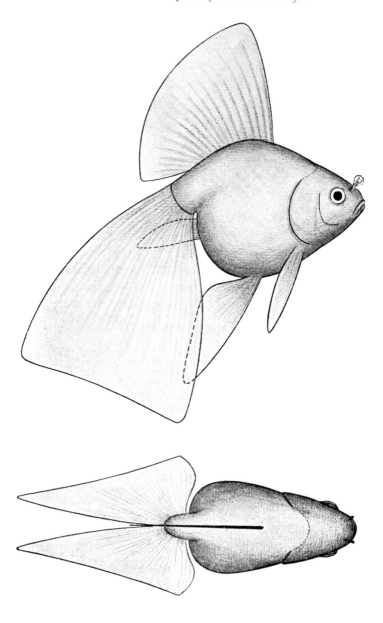

VEILTAIL (twintail)

Type Test

Fishes failing this test will be disqualified

1. Depth of body—greater than $\frac{2}{3}$ body length ($\frac{2}{3}$ L plus).
2. Caudal and anal fins—divided.
3. Minimum length of caudal fin—$\frac{3}{4}$ body length ($\frac{3}{4}$ L).
4. Trailing edge of caudal fin—having no apparent fork or pointed lobes.
5. Extremities of all fins—having rounded appearance.
6. Minimum length of body—$2\frac{1}{4}''$.

Standard Fishes

1. Depth of body—$\frac{3}{4}$ body length ($\frac{3}{4}$ L).
2. Caudal fin—$1\frac{1}{4}$ body length ($1\frac{1}{4}$ L).
3. Anterior margin of dorsal fin—$\frac{2}{3}$ body length ($\frac{2}{3}$ L).
4. Trailing edge of caudal fin—approximating to a straight line.
5. Length of pelvic fins—$\frac{3}{4}$ body length ($\frac{3}{4}$ L).

Points Table

Body				Fins		
D/L ratio	...	...	8	Contour and size of Dorsal ...		6
Dorsal contour (including nasal septum)		...	5	Contour and size of Caudal ...		8
Ventral contour	...	...	5	Contour and size of others ...		5
Lateral contour	...	...	3			—
Eyes and mouth	...	...	3			19
			—			—
			24			
			—			

Colour

Metallic Group				Other Groups (Calico)		
Orange	...	...	14	Blue		9
Silver ...	...	...	5	Orange or Yellow ...	...	5
			—	Black		5
			19			—
			—			19
Self-Orange			19			—
			—			

Condition and Deportment				Special Characteristic		
Condition	...	...	10	Development and contour of caudal fin		12
Deportment	...	...	9	Development and contour of dorsal fin		7
			—			—
			19			19
			—			—

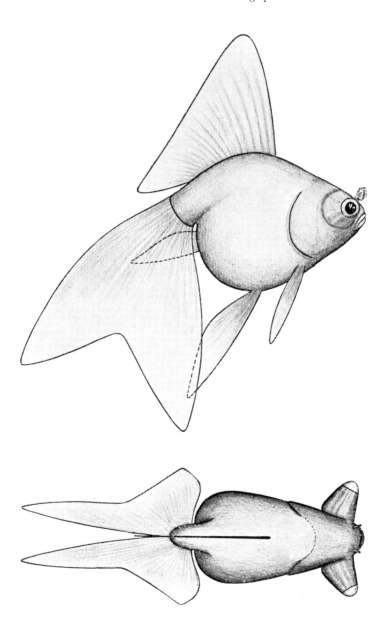

GLOBE-EYE

Type Test

Fishes failing this test will be disqualified

1. Depth of body—greater than $\frac{2}{3}$ body length ($\frac{2}{3}$ L).
2. Eyes—projecting from surface of head.
3. Caudal and anal fins—divided.
4. Trailing edge of caudal fin—having fork $\frac{1}{4}$ to $\frac{3}{8}$.
5. Minimum length of caudal fin $\frac{3}{4}$ body length ($\frac{3}{4}$ L).
6. Extremities of fins—having a pointed appearance.
7. Minimum length of body—$2\frac{1}{4}''$.

Standard Fishes

1. Depth of body—$\frac{3}{4}$ body length ($\frac{3}{4}$ L).
2. Eyes—projecting from surface of head to a marked degree.
3. Length of caudal fin—$1\frac{1}{4}$ body length ($1\frac{1}{4}$ L).
4. Anterior margin of dorsal fin—$\frac{2}{3}$ body length ($\frac{2}{3}$ L).
5. Trailing edge of caudal fin—depth of fork $\frac{1}{3}$.
6. Length of pelvic fins—$\frac{3}{4}$ body length ($\frac{3}{4}$ L).

Points Table

Body			Fins	
D/L ratio	8		Contour and size of Dorsal ...	6
Dorsal contour (including nasal septum)	5		Contour and size of Caudal ...	8
Ventral contour	5		Contour and size of others ...	5
Lateral contour	3			19
Eyes and mouth	3			
	24			

Colour

Metallic Group			Other Groups (Calico)			
Black (Moor)	19		Blue	9
	—		Orange or Yellow	5
	19		Black	5
				19

Condition and Deportment				Special Characteristic		
Condition	10		Eyes—Development	7
Deportment	9		,, Cornea	5
	—		,, Matching	4
	19		,, Colour	3
				19

Characteristic: Bramble appearance of head.

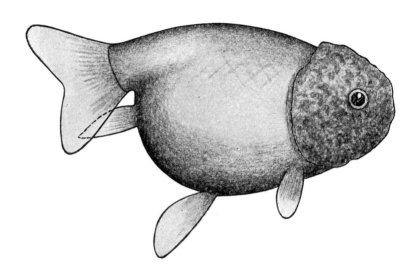

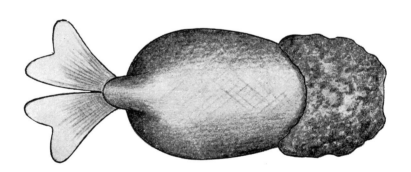

BRAMBLEHEAD (lionhead)

Type Test

Fishes failing this test will be disqualified

1. Depth of body—greater than $\frac{1}{2}$ body length ($\frac{1}{2}$ L plus).
2. Bramble—well developed.
3. Dorsal fin—absent.
4. Caudal and anal fins—divided.
5. Caudal fin—forked $\frac{1}{4}$ to $\frac{3}{8}$.
6. Extremities of fins—having a rounded appearance.
7. Minimum body length—$2\frac{1}{4}''$.

Standard Fishes

1. Depth of body—$\frac{3}{5}$ body length ($\frac{3}{5}$ L).
2. Bramble—to envelop the head.
3. Dorsal contour of trunk—an even curve.
4. Dorsal lobe of caudal fin—$\frac{1}{3}$ body length ($\frac{1}{3}$ L).
5. Caudal fin—forked $\frac{1}{3}$.
6. Pelvic fins—$\frac{1}{4}$ body length ($\frac{1}{4}$ L).

Points Table

Body				Fins	
D/L ratio	...	...	8	Contour and size of Caudal ...	8
Dorsal contour	...	...	5	Contour and size of others ...	5
Ventral contour	...	...	5	Contour of trunk in "dorsal	
Lateral contour	...	...	3	fin" region	6
Eyes and mouth	...	...	3		—
			—		19
			24		—

Colour

Metallic Group				Other Groups (Calico)	
Orange	...	...	14	Blue	9
Silver ...	...	...	5	Orange or Yellow	5
			—	Black	5
			19		—
			—		19
Self-Orange	...		19		—
			—		

Condition and Deportment				Special Characteristic	
Condition	...	...	10	*Bramble*	
Deportment	...	...	9	Development in cranial	
			—	region	9
			19	Development in infra-orbital	
			—	region	5
				Development in opercula	
				region	5
					—
					19
					—

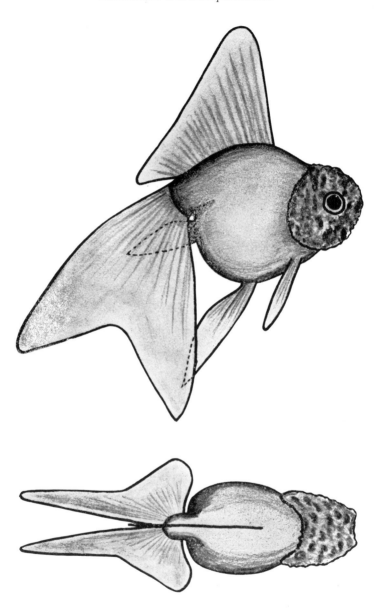

ORANDA

Type Test

Fishes failing this test will be disqualified

1. Depth of body—greater than $\frac{2}{3}$ body length ($\frac{2}{3}$ L).
2. Bramble—well developed.
3. Caudal and anal fins—divided.
4. Trailing edge of caudal fin—having fork $\frac{1}{4}$ to $\frac{3}{8}$.
5. Minimum length of caudal fin—$\frac{3}{4}$ body length ($\frac{3}{4}$ L).
6. Extremities of fins—having a pointed appearance.
7. Minimum length of body—$2\frac{1}{4}''$.

Standard Fishes

1. Depth of body—$\frac{3}{4}$ body length ($\frac{3}{4}$ L).
2. Bramble—to envelop the head.
3. Length of caudal fin—$1\frac{1}{4}$ body length ($1\frac{1}{4}$ L).
4. Anterior margin of dorsal fin—$\frac{2}{3}$ body length ($\frac{2}{3}$ L).
5. Trailing edge of caudal fin—depth of fork $\frac{1}{3}$.
6. Length of pelvic fins—$\frac{3}{4}$ body length ($\frac{3}{4}$ L).

Points Table

Body					Fins		
D/L ratio	...	...	...	8	Contour and size of Dorsal ...	6
Dorsal contour		...	...	5	Contour and size of Caudal ...	8
Ventral contour		...	...	5	Contour and size of others ...	5
Lateral contour		...	...	3		
Eyes and mouth		...	...	3		
				24		19

Colour

Metallic Group					Other Groups (Calico)		
Orange	...	...	...	14	Blue	...	...	...	...	9
Silver ...	...	...	...	5	Orange or Yellow	...	...	5
				19	Black ...	...	...	...	5
Self-Orange	...	...	...	19			19

Condition and Deportment					Special Characteristic	
Condition	...	...	...	10	*Bramble*	
Deportment	...	...	...	9	Development in cranial region	9
				19	Development in infra-orbital region	5
					Development in opercula region	5
						19

30

FANTAIL

Type Test

Fishes failing this test will be disqualified

1. Depth of body—greater than $\frac{3}{5}$ body length ($\frac{3}{5}$ L plus).
2. Caudal fin—dorsal lobe between $\frac{1}{3}$ and $\frac{1}{2}$ body length.
3. Caudal fin—divided and forked $\frac{1}{4}$ to $\frac{3}{8}$.
4. Caudal fin—upper ray not dropping below horizontal.
5. Anal fin—divided.
6. Extremities of fins—slightly rounded.
7. Minimum body length—$2\frac{1}{4}''$.

Standard Fishes

1. Depth of body—$\frac{2}{3}$ body length ($\frac{2}{3}$ L).
2. Anterior margin of dorsal fin—$\frac{1}{3}$ body length ($\frac{1}{3}$ L).
3. Caudal fin—forked $\frac{1}{3}$.
4. Caudal fin—rear view showing 60° at apex of fins.
5. Dorsal lobe of caudal fin—$\frac{2}{5}$ body length ($\frac{2}{5}$ L).
6. Dorsal lobe of caudal fin elevated at 35° approx.
7. Ventral lobe of caudal fin not to hang below level of lowest point of the body.
8. Pelvic fins—$\frac{1}{3}$ body length ($\frac{1}{3}$ L).

Points Table

Body

D/L ratio	...	... ...	8
Dorsal contour (including nasal septum)		... ...	5
Ventral contour	...	...	5
Lateral contour	...	...	3
Eyes and mouth	...	...	3
			24

Fins

Contour and size of Dorsal ...	6
Contour, size and rear view of Caudal	8
Contour and size of others ...	5
	19

Colour

Metallic Group

Orange	...	...	...	14
Silver ...	...	...	...	5
				19
Self-Orange	...	...	...	19

Other Groups (Calico)

Blue	...	...	...	9
Orange or Yellow	...	...	5
Black ...	...	...	...	5
				19

Condition and Deportment

Condition	...	...	...	10
Deportment	...	...	...	9
				19

Special Characteristic

Intensity of colour	...	...	7
Carriage of caudal fin	...	12
			19

Index